D0702052

Mix 'n' Match Meals in Minutes
for People with Diabetes SECOND EDITION

A NO-BRAINER SOLUTION to Meal Preparation
by Linda Gassenheimer

American Diabetes Association.

Cure • Care • Commitment®

Director, Book Publishing, Robert Anthony; *Managing Editor, Book Publishing,* Abe Ogden; *Editor,* Rebekah Renshaw; *Production Manager,* Melissa Sprott; *Composition,* ADA; *Cover Design,* Jennifer Sage; *Printer,* Victor Graphics, Inc.

©2003, 2008 by the American Diabetes Association, Inc. All Rights Reserved. No part of this publication may be reproduced or transmitted in any form or by any means, electronic or mechanical, including duplication, recording, or any information storage and retrieval system, without the prior written permission of the American Diabetes Association.

Printed in the United States of America
1 3 5 7 9 10 8 6 4 2

The suggestions and information contained in this publication are generally consistent with the Clinical Practice Recommendations and other policies of the American Diabetes Association, but they do not represent the policy or position of the Association or any of its boards or committees. Reasonable steps have been taken to ensure the accuracy of the information presented. However, the American Diabetes Association cannot ensure the safety or efficacy of any product or service described in this publication. Individuals are advised to consult a physician or other appropriate health care professional before undertaking any diet or exercise program or taking any medication referred to in this publication. Professionals must use and apply their own professional judgment, experience, and training and should not rely solely on the information contained in this publication before prescribing any diet, exercise, or medication. The American Diabetes Association—its officers, directors, employees, volunteers, and members—assumes no responsibility or liability for personal or other injury, loss, or damage that may result from the suggestions or information in this publication.

♾ The paper in this publication meets the requirements of the ANSI Standard Z39.48-1992 (permanence of paper).

ADA titles may be purchased for business or promotional use or for special sales. To purchase this book in large quantities, or for custom editions of this book with your logo, contact Special Sales & Promotions at the address below, or at booksales@diabetes.org or 703-299-2046.

American Diabetes Association
1701 North Beauregard Street
Alexandria, Virginia 22311

Library of Congress Cataloging-in-Publication Data

Gassenheimer, Linda.
   Mix 'n match meals in minutes for people with diabetes : a no-brainer solution to meal preparation / Linda Gassenheimer. — 2nd ed.
       p. cm.
   Includes bibliographical references and index.
   ISBN 978-1-58040-289-7 (alk. paper)
   1. Diabetes—Diet therapy—Recipes. I. Title.

RC662.G37 2007
641.5'6314--dc22

                                    2007044088

To my husband, Harold,
for his encouragement, help, and support.

Contents

Acknowledgments

Many thanks go to my husband, Harold. He has patiently edited every word and provided the analysis that helped structure these recipes.

Affectionate thank yous go to those whose guidance and support helped me to create this book:

My assistant, Jackie Murrill, who has been a wonderful help, spending hours with me testing recipes—and always with a smile.

Lynne Stein, Senior Program Manager for the American Diabetes Association in Miami, who encouraged me to write this book.

Maria Elena Torres, ARNP, MSN, CDE, and Marayxa Suarez, RD, LD, MS, CDE, educators whose infectious enthusiasm and guidance were an invaluable aid to understanding the issues faced by those with diabetes.

My editors, Sherrye Landrum and Laurie Guffey, whose support and friendship have made working on this book a delight.

My family, who always encourage my projects. My son James, his wife Patty, and their children, Zachary, Jacob, and Haley. My son John, his wife Jill, and their children, Jeffrey and Joanna. And my son Charles, his wife Lori, and their sons Daniel and Matthew. My sister Roberta and brother-in-law Robert, who helped to edit my thoughts and words.

Kathy Martin, my editor at the Miami Herald, who has enthusiastically encouraged my work.

Joseph Cooper and the management and staff at WLRN 91.3 FM, public radio for South Florida, for their friendship and help.

And all of you who use this book and prepare these meals: I hope you enjoy them as much as I've enjoyed creating these recipes!

Introduction

Several years ago, my sister called me, saying she had just come from the doctor's office with the news that she had type 2 diabetes. She bombarded me with questions: "What do I eat? Where do I start? What's on the list and what's off the list? How can I fit this style of eating into my busy life?"

Shortly after that, one of my friends called me. Her husband had just come home with the same news. Her questions were identical to my sister's. A dietitian at the hospital had given her some guidelines, but she needed to translate them into simple, quick meals. "What should I buy at the supermarket? How can I make tasty meals that will satisfy my husband?"

What my sister and friend—and perhaps you, too—need is a blueprint of what to have on hand, what to buy, and how to put ingredients together for quick, healthy, and delicious meals. I've provided a blueprint that is flexible, so you can mix and match your favorite meals, and structured, so you don't have to spend a lot of time planning what to serve. Diabetes doesn't mean broiled chicken every night—I've provided a wide variety of meals with many ethnic flavors. My main goal is for you to enjoy the recipes and know that you can still have delicious and exciting meals.

In this second edition of *Mix 'n' Match Meals in Minutes,* I have added a few new easy-to-follow recipes and made small changes in a few others to keep up with current diabetes nutrition guidelines. From years of training, I've learned to use classic techniques and familiar combinations to produce delicious results while cutting the cooking time. Some of these meals may take longer to prepare, but are worth the time when you have it. When you're in a hurry, just repeat one of the quick recipes you enjoy and save the longer ones for the weekend or another weekday meal.

New to this edition is a section on Speed Meals, where each meal can be prepared in less than 15 minutes, helping you make the most of your precious time. The recipes in this section use ingredients you can pick up in the supermarket and assemble at home in just minutes.

My method will save you time in the kitchen and at the grocery store. I've provided complete shopping lists, helpful hints, and a countdown section so you know exactly how to time your cooking so the whole meal is done at once. I developed these techniques after many years of juggling my family and career (founding and running a cooking school, guiding a gourmet supermarket, writing food columns for newspapers and magazines, and hosting a radio talk show), while still wanting to eat well!

Shopping List

I've arranged my list on how you buy food in the supermarket.

◆ Quick shopping is as important as quick cooking. You won't have to think about how many mushrooms to buy. I've given you the amount.

◆ I list the ingredients by supermarket departments to help you navigate the aisles with ease.

◆ Shopping lists will save you both time and money, since you buy only what you need.

◆ My staples list helps you organize your cabinets so they are not filled with unused items. To help you begin, I've included a list of all the staples I call for in the recipes on pages xiii–xiv. You probably already have many of these ingredients on hand and only need to buy a few fresh items.

Helpful Hints and Countdowns

Each meal contains tips on shopping, cooking, and substitutions and a countdown so you can get the whole meal on the table at the same time.

◆ You can hit the kitchen on the run without having to plan or think about each step.

◆ My prep times begin when I turn on the light in the kitchen and end when I bring the plates to the table.

◆ Helpful hints tell you what to buy, how to buy it, and what you can substitute. They include tips on the best preparation and quick-cooking techniques and how to save cleanup time.

Flexible Recipes

You can dress up these recipes for company, or dress them down to suit your budget.

- ◆ You can use the best sirloin, filet, or strip steak, or more economical cuts like flank and skirt steaks.

- ◆ You can use gourmet ingredients like infused olive oil or aged balsamic vinegar, or achieve delicious results with products you have on hand.

- ◆ When you choose a fish recipe, you can buy the freshest-looking fish in the market rather than the fish called for in the recipe.

- ◆ My flexible recipes let you choose whatever is in season, on sale, looks most appealing, or fits your mood.

As you go through the recipes, keep a few things in mind. All the recipes serve two people. You can use any type of oil and vinegar dressing, whole-wheat bread, and bran cereal you like, but the nutrient values may vary from those given. "Salt and pepper to taste" are NOT included in the analyses. Finally, a few of these recipes are high in sodium. If you need to watch your sodium levels, check those values carefully. These meals (any one breakfast, lunch, and dinner together) average about 1,350 calories and 165 grams of carbohydrate a day.

More Helpful Hints

Below are some general tips to help you eat well and cook like an expert!

Buying Tips

- ◆ Buy good-quality Parmesan cheese and ask the market to grate it for you or chop it in the food processor. Freeze extra for quick use. You can spoon out what you need and leave the rest frozen.

♦ Fresh fish should be firm to the touch and have a sweet smell. If it is whole, in addition to firm flesh, the eyes should be clear and the gills red.

♦ Buy shelled shrimp or ask for the shrimp to be shelled when you buy it. Many supermarkets will do this for a small fee. I find the slightly higher cost is worth the time saved.

♦ Buy tomato paste in a tube. You can use a small amount and the rest of the tube can be stored in the refrigerator until needed again.

♦ If you use dried herbs, make sure they are no more than six months old. They lose their flavor if kept too long.

♦ Brown rice takes about 45 minutes to cook, but there are several brands of quick-cooking brown rice available. Their cooking time ranges from 2 minutes to 30 minutes. You can use any quick-cooking rice and follow package cooking directions.

♦ I call for a small amount of wine, liquor, or liqueur in some recipes. If you don't have any on hand, you can buy small bottles or splits at most liquor stores.

Preparation Tips

♦ To quickly chop fresh herbs, wash and dry them and snip the leaves with scissors.

♦ To quickly peel ginger, scrape the skin away with the edge of a spoon.

♦ To quickly chop ginger, place small, peeled pieces in a garlic press with large holes. Press over a bowl to catch the juices.

Cooking Methods

Stir-Frying

♦ Make sure your wok is very hot before you add the ingredients.

♦ The secret to crisp, not steamed, stir-frying is to let the ingredients sit for about a minute when you add them to the hot wok before you toss them. This allows the wok to regain its heat after the cold ingredients have been added.

♦ For easy stir-frying, place all of the prepared ingredients on a cutting board or plate in order of use. You won't have to look at the recipe once you start to cook.

Cooking Fish

♦ Count 10 minutes cooking time for each inch of thickness. To check for doneness, stick the point of a knife into the flesh. If the flesh is opaque, it is ready.

♦ Remember the fish will continue to cook after it has been removed from the heat. Do not overcook, or the fish will be dry and tasteless.

Cooking Pasta

♦ Always use a very large pot. The pasta should be able to roll freely as it cooks.

♦ Make sure the water is at a rolling boil before you add the pasta.

♦ Add the pasta at one time and stir once.

Cooking Staples

Keep these foods on hand in your pantry or fridge, and you'll only have to pick up a few items at the supermarket to complete your meals.

DAIRY

Eggs   Butter
Parmesan cheese   Fat-free milk

GROCERY

Grains

Quick-cooking brown rice   Long-grain white rice

Spices

Salt

Chili powder

Ground cumin seed

Black peppercorns

Ground cinnamon

Breads and Cereals

Plain bread crumbs

Whole-wheat bread

Oatmeal

Bran cereal

Condiments

Reduced-fat mayonnaise

Dijon mustard

Ketchup

Hot pepper sauce

Worcestershire sauce

Lite soy sauce

Oils, Vinegars, and Dressings

Canola oil

Sesame oil

Olive oil

Reduced-fat oil and
    vinegar salad dressing

Balsamic vinegar

White vinegar

Cider vinegar

Oil and vinegar salad dressing

Vegetable oil cooking spray

Olive oil cooking spray

Miscellaneous

Sugar substitute

Raisins

Instant decaffeinated coffee

Vanilla extract

Extra-dry vermouth

Cornstarch

Fat-free reduced-sodium
    chicken broth

Orange juice

PRODUCE

Garlic

Red onion

Onion

Celery

Lemon

Carrots

Apples

A Month of Meals at a Glance

All of the breakfasts, lunches, and dinners can be mixed and matched according to your preference. Below is just one example of a tasty month of meals. I have organized them into a meal-at-a-glance chart, with some easy and quick meals midweek and those that take a little more time on the weekends. They are arranged to give variety throughout the day and over the days of the week.

Week 1	Sunday	Monday	Tuesday	Wednesday	Thursday	Friday	Saturday
Breakfast	Nutty Cinnamon French Toast, p. 30	Fluffy Scramble, p. 2	Spicy Grilled Cheese and Tomato Sandwich, p. 22	Breakfast Egg Sandwich, p. 20	Blueberry Smoothie with Tomato-Cheese Melt, p. 24	Toasted Turkey Breakfast Sandwich, p. 28	Green Pepper and Onion Frittata, p. 6
Lunch	Shrimp and Black-Eyed Pea Salad, p. 37	Italian Hero Sandwich, p. 59	Grilled Turkey Sausage, p. 61	Shrimp Roll, p. 63	Quick Turkey Wrap, p. 65	Tuscan Bean and Tuna Salad, p. 39	Antipasto Platter, p. 41
Dinner	Honey Mustard Beef Kabobs, p. 117	Baked Shrimp, p. 144	Chinese Steamed Fish, p. 147	Buffalo Chicken, p. 181	Chinese Pepper Steak, p. 120	Wok-Flashed Shrimp, p. 150	Korean Grilled Beef, p. 123

A Month of Meals at a Glance (continued)

Week 2	Sunday	Monday	Tuesday	Wednesday	Thursday	Friday	Saturday
Breakfast	Basque Red Pepper Frittata, p. 8	Spicy Grilled Cheese and Tomato Sandwich, p. 22	Microwave Ham-Scrambled Eggs, p. 4	Toasted Turkey Breakfast Sandwich, p. 28	Spinach and Mushroom Omelet, p. 16	Blueberry Smoothie with Tomato-Cheese Melt, p. 24	Norwegian Bagel Breakfast, p. 26
Lunch	Horace's Chickpea Soup, p. 83	Shrimp Caesar Salad, p. 43	Chicken Avocado Wrap, p. 67	Ham, Swiss, Apple, and Spinach Salad, p. 35	Mediterranean Egg Salad Sandwich, p. 69	Sausage and Tortellini Soup, p. 85	Smoked Fish Salad, p. 45
Dinner	Stuffed Veal Rolls, p. 129	Chinese Chicken with Cashew Nuts, p. 93	Italian Fish Soup, p. 153	Dijon Scallops, p. 195	Picadillo, p. 126	Crisp Thai Snapper, p. 159	Veal Gorgonzola, p. 132

A Month of Meals at a Glance (*continued*)

Week 3	Sunday	Monday	Tuesday	Wednesday	Thursday	Friday	Saturday
Breakfast	Smoked Salmon Omelet, p. 18	Fluffy Scramble, p. 2	Norwegian Bagel Breakfast, p. 26	Spicy Grilled Cheese and Tomato Sandwich, p. 22	Microwave Ham-Scrambled Eggs, p. 4	Toasted Turkey Breakfast Sandwich, p. 28	Tomato, Onion, and Basil Frittata, p. 10
Lunch	Steak and Portobello Mushroom Sandwich, p. 71	Turkey and Vegetable Soup, p. 87	Smoked Turkey Waldorf Salad, p. 47	Italian Peasant Salad, p. 49	Crunchy Coleslaw and Turkey Sandwich, p. 73	Roast Beef Sandwich, p. 75	Pasta and Bean Soup, p. 89
Dinner	Mojo Roasted Pork, p. 135	Southwestern Chicken, p. 96	Beef Supper Skillet, p. 213	Claudine's Tilapia, p. 156	Seafood Kabobs, p. 162	Cider Pork, p. 138	Three-Bean Chicken Toss, p. 191

A Month of Meals at a Glance (*continued*)

Week 4	Sunday	Monday	Tuesday	Wednesday	Thursday	Friday	Saturday
Breakfast	Spinach and Mushroom Omelet, p. 16	Toasted Turkey Breast Sandwich, p. 28	Gorgonzola Omelet, p. 14	Spicy Grilled Cheese and Tomato Sandwich, p. 22	Blueberry Smoothie with Tomato-Cheese Melt, p. 24	Swiss Omelet, p. 12	Nutty Cinnamon French Toast, p. 30
Lunch	Neapolitan Pizza, p. 77	Toasted Almond Chicken Salad, p. 51	Turkey and Refried Bean Enchiladas, p. 79	Salsa Beef Salad, p. 53	Chef's Salad, p. 55	Greek Tuna Salad Pita Pocket, p. 81	Tangy Chicken and Pear Salad, p. 57
Dinner	Shrimp Creole, p. 168	Mediterranean Meat Loaf, p. 105	Herb-Crusted Mahi-Mahi, p. 171	Key West Shrimp, p. 174	Pork and Apple Butter Sauce, p. 206	Turkey Chili, p. 111	Italian Roast Pork, p. 141

Breakfast

Eggs

Sandwiches 'n' Stuff

Fluffy Scramble

with Oatmeal

The secret to these light, fluffy scrambled eggs is whisking soft tofu into the eggs. A hint of cayenne pepper and Dijon mustard add a little bite.

Helpful Hint

◆ Soft tofu can be found in the refrigerated case of the produce section of most supermarkets.

Countdown

◆ Make oatmeal

◆ Toast bread

◆ Make eggs

SHOPPING LIST
PRODUCE
1 small package soft tofu

STAPLES
Eggs (4 needed)
Dijon mustard
Cayenne pepper
Oatmeal
Fat-free milk
Whole-wheat bread
Olive oil cooking spray
Salt
Black peppercorns

Nutrition Facts:
Fluffy Scramble

Exchanges/Choices
1 Starch
2 Lean Meat

Calories	185
Calories from Fat	67
Total Fat	7 g
Saturated Fat	2 g
Cholesterol	213 mg
Sodium	446 mg
Carbohydrate	15 g
Dietary Fiber	2 g
Sugars	4 g
Protein	15 g

Fluffy Scramble

Preparation time: 10 minutes
Serves 2/Serving size: 1/2 recipe

- 2 slices whole-wheat bread
  Olive oil cooking spray
- 2 whole eggs
- 2 egg whites
- 2 oz soft tofu (1/4 cup)
  Pinch cayenne pepper
- 1 Tbsp Dijon mustard
  Salt and freshly ground black pepper to taste

1. Toast bread. Spray one side of each slice with cooking spray and place on two plates.

2. Whisk whole eggs, egg whites, tofu, cayenne pepper, and mustard in a blender, food processor, or bowl. Add salt and pepper.

3. Heat a nonstick skillet over medium-high heat. Spray with cooking spray.

4. Add egg mixture and scramble eggs 1 minute. Remove and serve on toasted bread.

Nutrition Facts:
Oatmeal

Exchanges/Choices
1 1/2 Starch
1/2 Fat-Free Milk

Calories	150
Calories from Fat	20
Total Fat	2 g
Saturated Fat	0.4 g
Cholesterol	0 mg
Sodium	70 mg
Carbohydrate	25 g
Dietary Fiber	3 g
Sugars	6 g
Protein	9 g

Oatmeal

Preparation time: 5 minutes
Serves 2/Serving size: 1/2 cup

- 2/3 cup oatmeal
  cup water
- 1 cup fat-free milk

1. Place oatmeal in a microwave-safe bowl and add water.

2. Microwave on high 3 minutes.

3. Place in two bowls and serve with milk.

Microwave Ham-Scrambled Eggs

with Oatmeal

Scrambled eggs and ham in less than 3 minutes and no pan to wash! It's easy with this recipe.

Helpful Hint

♦ Microwave timing may vary with different microwave ovens, so change your timing accordingly.

Countdown

♦ Make oatmeal

♦ Make eggs

♦ Toast bread

SHOPPING LIST

DELI
1 small package lean ham

STAPLES
Eggs (6 needed)
Whole-wheat bread
Oatmeal
Fat-free milk
Salt
Black peppercorns

Microwave Ham-Scrambled Eggs

Nutrition Facts:
Microwave Ham-Scrambled Eggs

Exchanges/Choices
2 Starch
2 Lean Meat
1/2 Fat

Calories	291
Calories from Fat	81
Total Fat	9 g
Saturated Fat	2 g
Cholesterol	229 mg
Sodium	845 mg
Carbohydrate	27 g
Dietary Fiber	4 g
Sugars	4 g
Protein	26 g

Preparation time: 10 minutes
Serves 2/Serving size: 1/2 recipe

> 2 eggs
> 4 egg whites
> 2 oz lean ham torn into bite-sized pieces (1/2 cup)
> Salt and freshly ground black pepper to taste
> 4 slices whole-wheat bread

1. Mix 1 whole egg, 2 egg whites, and half the ham pieces together in a microwave-safe bowl; repeat with remaining ingredients in a second bowl.

2. Add salt and pepper to both.

3. Microwave first bowl on high for 1 minute. Stir and return for 30 seconds; repeat with second serving.

4. Toast bread and serve with ham and eggs.

Oatmeal

Nutrition Facts:
Oatmeal

Exchanges/Choices
1 1/2 Starch
1/2 Fat-Free Milk

Calories	150
Calories from Fat	20
Total Fat	2 g
Saturated Fat	0.4 g
Cholesterol	0 mg
Sodium	70 mg
Carbohydrate	25 g
Dietary Fiber	3 g
Sugars	6 g
Protein	9 g

Preparation time: 5 minutes
Serves 2/Serving size: 1/2 cup

> 2/3 cup oatmeal
> cup water
> 1 cup fat-free milk

1. Place oatmeal in a microwave-safe bowl and add water.

2. Microwave on high 3 minutes.

3. Place in two bowls and serve with milk.

Green Pepper and Onion Frittata

with Oatmeal

Plump, flavorful frittatas make a nice breakfast change. They take a little longer to make than scrambled eggs or omelets. Make them on the weekend or make them the night before and heat them in the microwave the next morning.

Frittatas and omelets are different. A frittata is cooked very slowly over low heat, making it firm and set, while an omelet is cooked fast over high heat, making it creamy and runny. A frittata needs to be cooked on both sides. Some people flip it in the pan. A much easier way is to place it under a broiler for half a minute. Here are a few variations for you to try.

Helpful Hints

◆ Buy chopped or diced frozen green pepper and onion for this recipe.

◆ If frozen onion and green pepper are not available, use fresh and cook them in a microwave for 4 minutes before using them in the frittata.

◆ To defrost onion and green pepper, place both in a microwave-safe bowl and microwave for 1 minute.

Countdown

◆ Make toast

◆ Preheat broiler

◆ Make frittata

◆ Make oatmeal

SHOPPING LIST
GROCERY
Frozen chopped onion
Frozen chopped green bell pepper

STAPLES
Eggs (6 needed)
Whole-wheat bread
Oatmeal
Fat-free milk
Olive oil spray
Salt
Black peppercorns

Green Pepper and Onion Frittata

Preparation time: 20 minutes ♦ **Serves 2/Serving size : 1/2 recipe**

2 slices whole-wheat bread (about 1 oz each)
   Olive oil spray
2 whole eggs
4 egg whites
1 cup frozen chopped onion, defrosted
1 cup frozen chopped green bell pepper, defrosted
   Salt and freshly ground black pepper

1. Toast bread and spray one side of each slice with olive oil spray.

2. Mix whole eggs, egg whites, onion, and green pepper together. Add salt and pepper to taste.

3. Heat a 9- to 10-inch nonstick skillet over medium-low heat and spray with olive oil spray. Add the egg mixture and turn the heat down to low.

4. Preheat broiler.

5. Cook without browning the bottom 10 minutes. The eggs will be set, but the top will be a little runny.

6. Place pan under the broiler for 30 seconds to 1 minute until the top is set, but not brown. Remove and cut in half. Slide halves onto two plates and serve with toast.

Nutrition Facts: Green Pepper and Onion Fritatta

Exchanges/Choices
1 Starch
2 Vegetable
2 Lean Meat
1/2 Fat

Calories	225
Calories from Fat	55
Total Fat	6 g
Saturated Fat	1.8 g
Cholesterol	210 mg
Sodium	315 mg
Carbohydrate	24 g
Dietary Fiber	4 g
Sugars	8 g
Protein	18 g

Oatmeal

Preparation time: 5 minutes
Serves 2/Serving size: 1/2 cup

2/3 cup oatmeal
     cup water
1   cup fat-free milk

1. Place oatmeal in a microwave-safe bowl and add water.

2. Microwave on high 3 minutes.

3. Place in two bowls and serve with milk.

Nutrition Facts: Oatmeal

Exchanges/Choices
1 1/2 Starch
1/2 Fat-Free Milk

Calories	150
Calories from Fat	20
Total Fat	2 g
Saturated Fat	0.4 g
Cholesterol	0 mg
Sodium	70 mg
Carbohydrate	25 g
Dietary Fiber	3 g
Sugars	6 g
Protein	9 g

Basque Red Pepper Frittata

with Oatmeal

Countdown

◆ Microwave vegetables

◆ Make toast

◆ Preheat broiler

◆ Make frittata

◆ Make oatmeal

SHOPPING LIST

PRODUCE
1 large red bell pepper
2 plum tomatoes

STAPLES
Eggs (6 needed)
Garlic
Whole-wheat bread
Oatmeal
Fat-free milk
Olive oil cooking spray
Salt
Black peppercorns

Nutrition Facts:
Basque Red Pepper Frittata

Exchanges/Choices
1 Starch
1 Vegetable
2 Lean Meat

Calories	215
Calories from Fat	59
Total Fat	7 g
Saturated Fat	2 g
Cholesterol	213 mg
Sodium	331 mg
Carbohydrate	23 g
Dietary Fiber	4 g
Sugars	7 g
Protein	17 g

Basque Red Pepper Frittata

Preparation time: 20 minutes
Serves 2/Serving size: 1/2 recipe

- 1 cup thinly sliced red bell peppers
- 2 plum tomatoes, thinly sliced
- 2 medium cloves garlic, crushed
- 2 slices whole-wheat bread
  Olive oil cooking spray
- 2 whole eggs
- 4 egg whites
  Salt and freshly ground black pepper to taste

1. Place red peppers, tomatoes, and garlic in a microwave-safe bowl. Microwave on high 5 minutes.

2. Meanwhile, toast bread and spray one side of each slice with olive oil cooking spray. Set aside.

3. Preheat broiler. Mix whole eggs and egg whites together. Add vegetables, salt, and pepper.

4. Heat a 9- to 10-inch nonstick skillet over medium-low heat and spray with olive oil cooking spray. Add egg mixture and turn the heat down to low.

5. Cook without browning the bottom 10 minutes. The eggs will be set, but the top will be a little runny.

6. Place pan under the broiler for 30 seconds to 1 minute until the top is set, but not brown. Remove and cut in half. Slide halves onto two plates and serve with toast.

Nutrition Facts:
Oatmeal

Exchanges/Choices
1 1/2 Starch
1/2 Fat-Free Milk

Calories	150
Calories from Fat	20
Total Fat	2 g
Saturated Fat	0.4 g
Cholesterol	0 mg
Sodium	70 mg
Carbohydrate	25 g
Dietary Fiber	3 g
Sugars	6 g
Protein	9 g

Oatmeal

Preparation time: 5 minutes
Serves 2/Serving size: 1/2 cup

- 2/3 cup oatmeal
  cup water
- 1 cup fat-free milk

1. Place oatmeal in a microwave-safe bowl and add water.

2. Microwave on high 3 minutes.

3. Place in two bowls and serve with milk.

Tomato, Onion, and Basil Frittata

with Oatmeal

Countdown

♦ Microwave vegetables

♦ Make toast

♦ Preheat broiler

♦ Make frittata

♦ Make oatmeal

SHOPPING LIST

PRODUCE
1 red onion
1 small bunch basil

GROCERY
1 small can whole tomatoes

STAPLES
Eggs (6 needed)
Whole-wheat bread
Olive oil cooking spray
Oatmeal
Fat-free milk
Salt
Black peppercorns

Nutrition Facts:
Tomato, Onion, and
Basil Frittata

Exchanges/Choices
1 Starch
1 Vegetable
2 Lean Meat

Calories	231
Calories from Fat	58
Total Fat	6 g
Saturated Fat	2 g
Cholesterol	213 mg
Sodium	500 mg
Carbohydrate	25 g
Dietary Fiber	5 g
Sugars	9 g
Protein	19 g

Tomato, Onion, and Basil Frittata

Preparation time: 20 minutes
Serves 2/Serving size: 1/2 recipe

1 cup thinly sliced red onion
1 cup canned whole tomatoes, drained
1 cup fresh basil leaves, torn into bite-sized pieces
2 slices whole-wheat bread
  Olive oil cooking spray
2 whole eggs
4 egg whites
  Salt and freshly ground black pepper to taste

1. Place onion and tomatoes in a microwave-safe bowl. Break up the tomatoes with the edge of a spoon. Microwave on high 5 minutes. Remove from microwave and add basil.

2. Toast bread and spray one side of each slice with cooking spray.

3. Preheat broiler. Mix whole eggs and egg whites together. Add onion, tomatoes, salt, and pepper.

4. Heat a 9- to 10-inch nonstick skillet over medium-low heat. Add egg mixture and turn the heat down to low.

5. Cook without browning the bottom 10 minutes. The eggs will be set, but the top will be a little runny.

6. Place pan under the broiler for 30 seconds to 1 minute until the top is set, but not brown. Remove and cut in half. Slide halves onto two plates and serve with toast.

Oatmeal

Preparation time: 5 minutes
Serves 2/Serving size: 1/2 cup

2/3 cup oatmeal
    cup water
1 cup fat-free milk

1. Place oatmeal in a microwave-safe bowl and add water.

2. Microwave on high 3 minutes.

3. Place in two bowls and serve with milk.

Nutrition Facts:
Oatmeal

Exchanges/Choices
1 1/2 Starch
1/2 Fat-Free Milk

Calories	150
Calories from Fat	20
Total Fat	2 g
Saturated Fat	0.4 g
Cholesterol	0 mg
Sodium	70 mg
Carbohydrate	25 g
Dietary Fiber	3 g
Sugars	6 g
Protein	9 g

Swiss Omelet

with Bran Cereal

A perfect omelet is golden on the top with a delicate creamy center. The secret is to cook it over medium-high heat for only a couple of minutes. Here is a basic cheese omelet recipe followed by several variations.

Helpful Hint

♦ Slightly shake the pan while the omelet cooks to help set all of the egg. This also helps make the omelet a little thicker.

Countdown

♦ Toast bread

♦ Make omelet

♦ Assemble cereal

SHOPPING LIST

DAIRY
2 oz reduced-fat Swiss cheese

GROCERY
Rye bread

STAPLES

Cayenne pepper
Egg substitute
Olive oil cooking spray
Bran cereal
Fat-free milk
Salt
Black peppercorns

Nutrition Facts:
Swiss Omelet

Exchanges/Choices
1 Starch
5 Lean Meat

Calories	257
Calories from Fat	40
Total Fat	4 g
Saturated Fat	2 g
Cholesterol	10 mg
Sodium	761 mg
Carbohydrate	17 g
Dietary Fiber	2 g
Sugars	3 g
Protein	35 g

Swiss Omelet

Preparation time: 10 minutes
Serves 2/Serving size: 1/2 recipe

> 2 slices rye bread
> Olive oil cooking spray
> 2 cups egg substitute
> Pinch cayenne pepper
> Salt and freshly ground black pepper to taste
> 2 oz reduced-fat Swiss cheese torn into bite-sized pieces (1/2 cup)

1. Toast bread and spray one side of each slice with olive oil cooking spray. Set aside.

2. Pour egg substitute into a bowl and stir in cayenne pepper, salt, and pepper.

3. Heat a 9- to 10-inch nonstick skillet over medium-high heat and spray with cooking spray. Pour in egg mixture. Let eggs set for about 30 seconds. Tip the pan and lightly move the eggs so that they all set. Cook 1 1/2 minutes or until eggs are set. Cook a few seconds longer for firmer eggs.

4. Place the cheese on half the omelet and fold the omelet in half. Slide out of the pan by tipping the pan and holding a plate vertically against the side of the pan. Invert the omelet onto the plate.

5. Cut in half and serve with toast.

Nutrition Facts:
Bran Cereal

Exchanges/Choices
2 Starch
1/2 Fat-Free Milk

Calories	167
Calories from Fat	12
Total Fat	1 g
Saturated Fat	0 g
Cholesterol	2 mg
Sodium	363 mg
Carbohydrate	42 g
Dietary Fiber	18 g
Sugars	17 g
Protein	8 g

Bran Cereal

Preparation time: 2 minutes
Serves 2/Serving size: 1/2 recipe

> 1 cup bran cereal
> 1 cup fat-free milk

1. Pour cereal into two bowls and pour milk on top.

Gorgonzola Omelet
with Bran Cereal

Helpful Hint

◆ Domestic crumbled Gorgonzola can be found in the dairy case of most supermarkets. You can use any type of blue cheese in this recipe.

Countdown

◆ Toast bread

◆ Make omelet

◆ Assemble cereal

SHOPPING LIST

DAIRY
1 oz crumbled Gorgonzola cheese

GROCERY
Rye bread

STAPLES
Cayenne pepper
Egg substitute
Olive oil cooking spray
Bran cereal
Fat-free milk
Salt
Black peppercorns

Nutrition Facts:
Gorgonzola Omelet

Exchanges/Choices
1 Starch
4 Lean Meat
1/2 Fat

Calories	237
Calories from Fat	45
Total Fat	5 g
Saturated Fat	3 g
Cholesterol	11 mg
Sodium	829 mg
Carbohydrate	17 g
Dietary Fiber	2 g
Sugars	3 g
Protein	29 g

Gorgonzola Omelet

Preparation time: 10 minutes
Serves 2/Serving size: 1/2 recipe

> 2 slices rye bread
> Olive oil cooking spray
> 2 cups egg substitute
> Pinch cayenne pepper
> Salt and freshly ground black pepper to taste
> 1 oz crumbled Gorgonzola (1/3 cup)

1. Toast bread and spray one side of each slice with olive oil cooking spray. Set aside.

2. Pour egg substitute in a bowl and stir in cayenne pepper, salt, and pepper.

3. Heat a 9- to 10-inch nonstick skillet over medium-high heat and spray with cooking spray. Pour in egg mixture. Let the eggs set for about 30 seconds. Tip the pan and lightly move the eggs so that they all set. Cook 1 1/2 minutes or until eggs are set. Cook a few seconds longer for firmer eggs.

4. Place the cheese on half the omelet and fold the omelet in half. Slide out of the pan by tipping the pan and holding a plate vertically against the side of the pan. Invert the omelet onto the plate.

5. Cut in half and serve with toast.

Nutrition Facts:
Bran Cereal

Exchanges/Choices
2 Starch
1/2 Fat-Free Milk

Calories	167
Calories from Fat	12
Total Fat	1 g
Saturated Fat	0 g
Cholesterol	2 mg
Sodium	363 mg
Carbohydrate	42 g
Dietary Fiber	18 g
Sugars	17 g
Protein	8 g

Bran Cereal

Preparation time: 2 minutes
Serves 2/Serving size: 1/2 recipe

> 1 cup bran cereal
> 1 cup fat-free milk

1. Pour cereal into two bowls and pour milk on top.

Spinach and Mushroom Omelet

with Bran Cereal

Helpful Hints

◆ If you do not have a microwave oven, place the spinach in a saucepan without water, cover, and cook 3–4 minutes. Drain and add mushrooms, then sauté 1 minute.

◆ If mushroom slices are large, cut them in half.

Countdown

◆ Make filling

◆ Toast bread

◆ Complete omelet

◆ Assemble cereal

SHOPPING LIST

PRODUCE
1 bag washed ready-to-eat spinach
1/4 lb portobello mushrooms

GROCERY
Ground nutmeg
Rye bread

STAPLES
Egg substitute
Olive oil cooking spray
Bran cereal
Fat-free milk
Salt
Black peppercorns

Nutrition Facts:
Spinach and
Mushroom Omelet

Exchanges/Choices
1 Starch
1 Vegetable
3 Lean Meat

Calories	205
Calories from Fat	11
Total Fat	1 g
Saturated Fat	0 g
Cholesterol	0 mg
Sodium	646 mg
Carbohydrate	20 g
Dietary Fiber	3 g
Sugars	3 g
Protein	28 g

Spinach and Mushroom Omelet

Preparation time: 10 minutes
Serves 2/Serving size: 1/2 recipe

> 1 cup washed ready-to-eat spinach
> 1 1/2 cups sliced portobello mushrooms (1/4 lb)
> 1/8 tsp nutmeg
> 2 slices rye bread
> Olive oil cooking spray
> 2 cups egg substitute
> Salt and freshly ground black pepper to taste

1. Place spinach and mushrooms in a microwave-safe bowl. Sprinkle with nutmeg and microwave on high for 3 minutes.

2. Toast bread and spray one side of each slice with olive oil cooking spray. Set aside.

3. Pour egg substitute into a bowl and add salt and pepper.

4. Heat a 9- to 10-inch nonstick skillet over medium-high heat and spray with cooking spray. Pour in egg mixture and let eggs set for 30 seconds. Tip the pan and lightly move the eggs so that they all set. Cook 1 1/2 minutes or until eggs are set. Cook a few seconds longer for firmer eggs.

5. Place spinach mixture on half the omelet and fold the omelet in half. Slide out of the pan by tipping the pan and holding a plate vertically against the side of the pan. Invert the omelet onto the plate.

6. Cut in half and serve with toast.

Nutrition Facts:
Bran Cereal

Exchanges/Choices
2 Starch
1/2 Fat-Free Milk

Calories	167
Calories from Fat	12
Total Fat	1 g
Saturated Fat	0 g
Cholesterol	2 mg
Sodium	363 mg
Carbohydrate	42 g
Dietary Fiber	18 g
Sugars	17 g
Protein	8 g

Bran Cereal

Preparation time: 2 minutes
Serves 2/Serving size: 1/2 recipe

> 1 cup bran cereal
> 1 cup fat-free milk

1. Pour cereal into two bowls and pour milk on top.

Smoked Salmon Omelet

with Bran Cereal

This is a great way to use leftover smoked salmon.

Countdown

◆ Toast bread

◆ Make omelet

◆ Assemble cereal

SHOPPING LIST

DAIRY
1 small carton fat-free ricotta cheese

DELI
2 oz smoked salmon

GROCERY
Dried dill
Rye bread

STAPLES

Egg substitute
Olive oil cooking spray
Bran cereal
Fat-free milk
Salt
Black peppercorns

Smoked Salmon Omelet

Preparation time: 10 minutes
Serves 2/Serving size: 1/2 recipe

Nutrition Facts:
Smoked Salmon Omelet

Exchanges/Choices
1 Starch
4 Lean Meat

Calories	231
Calories from Fat	19
Total Fat	2 g
Saturated Fat	0 g
Cholesterol	12 mg
Sodium	866 mg
Carbohydrate	17 g
Dietary Fiber	2 g
Sugars	3 g
Protein	33 g

- 2 slices rye bread
  Olive oil cooking spray
- 2 oz smoked salmon, cut into 1-inch pieces (1/3 cup)
- 2 Tbsp fat-free ricotta cheese
- 1 tsp dried dill
- 2 cups egg substitute
  Salt and freshly ground black pepper to taste

1. Toast bread and spray one side of each slice with olive oil cooking spray. Set aside.

2. Mix salmon, ricotta cheese, and dill together.

3. Pour egg substitute into a bowl and add salt and pepper.

4. Heat a 9- to 10-inch nonstick skillet over medium-high heat and spray with cooking spray. Pour in egg mixture and let eggs set for 30 seconds. Tip the pan and lightly move the eggs so that they all set. Cook 1 1/2 minutes or until eggs are set. Cook a few seconds longer for firmer eggs.

5. Place the salmon mixture on half the omelet and fold the omelet in half. Slide out of the pan by tipping the pan and holding a plate vertically against the side of the pan. Invert the omelet onto the plate.

6. Cut in half and serve with toast.

Bran Cereal

Preparation time: 2 minutes
Serves 2/Serving size: 1/2 recipe

Nutrition Facts:
Bran Cereal

Exchanges/Choices
2 Starch
1/2 Fat-Free Milk

Calories	167
Calories from Fat	12
Total Fat	1 g
Saturated Fat	0 g
Cholesterol	2 mg
Sodium	363 mg
Carbohydrate	42 g
Dietary Fiber	18 g
Sugars	17 g
Protein	8 g

- 1 cup bran cereal
- 1 cup fat-free milk

1. Pour cereal into two bowls and pour milk on top.

Breakfast Egg Sandwich

with Oatmeal

This is a quick egg dish that you can take on the run. You can make the egg the night before and assemble the sandwich the next morning.

Helpful Hint

◆ To flip the cooked egg pancake over quickly, cut it in half and flip each side separately. Or, place the pan under a broiler for a few seconds to cook the top.

Countdown

◆ Make oatmeal

◆ Make eggs

◆ Toast bread

◆ Assemble sandwich

SHOPPING LIST

DELI
1 small package lean ham

STAPLES —
Eggs (6 needed)
Whole-wheat bread
Olive oil cooking spray
Oatmeal
Fat-free milk
Salt
Black peppercorns

Nutrition Facts:
Breakfast Egg Sandwich

Exchanges/Choices
2 Starch
2 Lean Meat
1/2 Fat

Calories	291
Calories from Fat	81
Total Fat	9 g
Saturated Fat	3 g
Cholesterol	229 mg
Sodium	844 mg
Carbohydrate	27 g
Dietary Fiber	4 g
Sugars	4 g
Protein	26 g

Breakfast Egg Sandwich

Preparation time: 15 minutes
Serves 2/Serving size: 1 sandwich

- 2 whole eggs
- 4 egg whites
- 2 oz lean ham, torn into bite-sized pieces (1/2 cup)
  Salt and freshly ground black pepper to taste
  Olive oil cooking spray
- 4 slices whole-wheat bread

1. Whisk together whole eggs and egg whites.

2. Stir in ham, salt, and pepper.

3. Heat a medium-size nonstick skillet over medium heat, spray with cooking spray, and add the egg mixture. Let sit for 3 to 4 minutes without stirring. Flip eggs over and cook 30 seconds.

4. Toast bread and spray one side of each slice with cooking spray. Divide eggs in half. Fold each half in half to fit in between the two bread slices, sprayed sides in.

Nutrition Facts:
Oatmeal

Exchanges/Choices
1 1/2 Starch
1/2 Fat-Free Milk

Calories	150
Calories from Fat	20
Total Fat	2 g
Saturated Fat	0.4 g
Cholesterol	0 mg
Sodium	70 mg
Carbohydrate	25 g
Dietary Fiber	3 g
Sugars	6 g
Protein	9 g

Oatmeal

Preparation time: 5 minutes
Serves 2/Serving size: 1/2 cup

- 2/3 cup oatmeal
- cup water
- 1 cup fat-free milk

1. Place oatmeal in a microwave-safe bowl and add water.

2. Microwave on high 3 minutes.

3. Place in two bowls and serve with milk.

Spicy Grilled Cheese and Tomato Sandwich

with Oatmeal

Creamy melted cheese with a hint of hot pepper and topped with sliced tomatoes is one of my husband's favorite quick breakfasts.

Helpful Hint

◆ Look for a reduced-fat cheddar cheese that contains no more than 1.5 g saturated fat (an example is Cabot Vermont 75% light brand cheddar cheese). Look for a brand that melts well.

Countdown

◆ Prepare ingredients

◆ Heat in toaster oven or under broiler

SHOPPING LIST

DELI
4 oz low-sodium turkey breast

PRODUCE
1 small tomato

DAIRY
1 small package reduced-fat cheddar cheese

GROCERY
Dry mustard

STAPLES
Dijon mustard
Cayenne pepper
Oatmeal
Fat-free milk
Whole-wheat bread

Nutrition Facts:
Spicy Grilled Cheese and Tomato Sandwich

Exchanges/Choices
2 Starch
3 Lean Meat

Calories	295
Calories from Fat	45
Total Fat	5 g
Saturated Fat	2 g
Cholesterol	55 mg
Sodium	495 mg
Carbohydrate	26 g
Dietary Fiber	5 g
Sugars	5 g
Protein	34 g

Spicy Grilled Cheese and Tomato Sandwich

Preparation time: 10 minutes
Serves: 2/Serving size: 1 sandwich

4 oz cooked turkey breast (with no added salt)
2 oz sliced reduced-fat cheddar cheese
4 slices whole-wheat bread (about 1 oz each)
2 tsp dry mustard
   Pinch cayenne pepper
1 small tomato, sliced (approximately 4 oz)

1. Place turkey and cheese on bread slices and sprinkle dry mustard and cayenne pepper on top.

2. Place tomato slices on top and toast or place under a broiler for 1 minute or until cheese melts.

Nutrition Facts:
Oatmeal

Exchanges/Choices
1 1/2 Starch
1/2 Fat-Free Milk

Calories	150
Calories from Fat	20
Total Fat	2 g
Saturated Fat	0.4 g
Cholesterol	0 mg
Sodium	70 mg
Carbohydrate	25 g
Dietary Fiber	3 g
Sugars	6 g
Protein	9 g

Oatmeal

Preparation time: 5 minutes
Serves 2/Serving size: 1/2 cup

2/3 cup oatmeal
   cup water
1 cup fat-free milk

1. Place oatmeal in a microwave-safe bowl and add water.

2. Microwave on high 3 minutes.

3. Place in two bowls and serve with milk.

Blueberry Smoothie

with Tomato-Cheese Melt and Bran Cereal

Rich, smooth, and easy to drink, smoothies are perfect for quick breakfasts. Many take-out smoothies are very high in carbohydrates. This one is not. It takes only minutes to make and tastes great!

Helpful Hints

◆ You can use frozen or fresh blueberries in this recipe, but make sure the frozen ones are not packed in sugar syrup.

◆ If you use frozen blueberries, your smoothie may be very thick. Add a little water to thin.

◆ You can use any type of reduced-fat cheese in this sandwich, but look for a brand that melts well.

Countdown

◆ Make smoothie

◆ Make sandwich

◆ Assemble cereal

SHOPPING LIST

PRODUCE
1 small carton blueberries or
   frozen blueberries
1 small tomato

DAIRY
8 oz fat-free artificially sweetened
   blueberry yogurt
1 small package shredded reduced-fat
   cheddar cheese

STAPLES
Whole-wheat bread
Sugar substitute
Bran cereal
Fat-free milk

Nutrition Facts:
Blueberry Smoothie

Exchanges/Choices
1/2 Fruit
1 Fat-Free Milk

Calories	104
Calories from Fat	2
Total Fat	0 g
Saturated Fat	0 g
Cholesterol	2 mg
Sodium	64 mg
Carbohydrate	22 g
Dietary Fiber	2 g
Sugars	14 g
Protein	4 g

Blueberry Smoothie

Preparation time: 5 minutes
Serves 2/Serving size: 1/2 recipe

- 1 cup blueberries
- 8 oz fat-free artificially sweetened blueberry yogurt
  Sugar substitute equivalent to 2 tsp sugar
- 3 cups ice cubes

1. Place blueberries and yogurt in a blender and blend until smooth.

2. Add sugar substitute and ice and blend until thick.

Nutrition Facts:
Tomato-Cheese Melt

Exchanges/Choices
1 Starch
1/2 Fat

Calories	100
Calories from Fat	20
Total Fat	3 g
Saturated Fat	1 g
Cholesterol	5 mg
Sodium	213 mg
Carbohydrate	15 g
Dietary Fiber	2 g
Sugars	3 g
Protein	5 g

Tomato-Cheese Melt

Preparation time: 5 minutes
Serves 2/Serving size: 1/2 recipe

- 2 slices whole-wheat bread
- 2 Tbsp shredded reduced-fat cheddar cheese
- 1 small tomato, sliced

1. Sprinkle cheese on bread slices.

2. Top with tomato slices and place in toaster oven or under broiler for 2–3 minutes or until cheese melts.

3. Serve with smoothie.

Bran Cereal

Nutrition Facts:
Bran Cereal

See page 27 for nutritional information.

Preparation time: 2 minutes
Serves 2/Serving size: 1/2 recipe

- 1 cup bran cereal
- 1 cup fat-free milk

1. Pour cereal into two bowls and pour milk on top.

Norwegian Bagel Breakfast

with Bran Cereal

Bagels come in all sizes. For this recipe, choose one that is about the size of a coffee can lid.

Helpful Hints

◆ To quickly chop fresh dill, wash, dry, and snip the leaves with scissors right off the stem.

◆ If using dried dill, make sure the leaves are still green in the bottle for the best flavor. When they turn gray or brown, it's time for a new bottle.

◆ You can use smoked salmon in this recipe, but it's higher in fat than other smoked fish.

Countdown

◆ Assemble cereal

◆ Make bagel breakfast

SHOPPING LIST

PRODUCE
2 medium tomatoes
1 medium cucumber
1 small bunch fresh dill (or dried dill)

DELI
6 oz smoked fish (white fish,
    haddock, salmon, or mackerel)

GROCERY
1 small bagel

STAPLES

Butter
Black peppercorns
Bran cereal
Fat-free milk

Nutrition Facts:
Norwegian Bagel Breakfast

Exchanges/Choices
1 Starch
2 Vegetable
3 Lean Meat
1 Fat

Calories	278
Calories from Fat	52
Total Fat	**6 g**
Saturated Fat	3 g
Cholesterol	**75 mg**
Sodium	**893 mg**
Carbohydrate	**29 g**
Dietary Fiber	3 g
Sugars	8 g
Protein	**27 g**

Norwegian Bagel Breakfast

Preparation time: 5 minutes
Serves 2/Serving size: 1/2 recipe

- 2 Tbsp fresh snipped dill (or 1 tsp dried dill)
- 2 tsp butter
- 1 small bagel (about 3 inches in diameter)
- 2 medium tomatoes, thinly sliced
- 1 medium cucumber, thinly sliced
- 6 oz smoked fish (white fish, haddock, salmon or mackerel)
  Freshly ground black pepper to taste

1. Mix dill and butter together.

2. Slice bagel in half, spread with dill butter, and toast in toaster oven or under broiler.

3. Divide tomato slices, cucumber, and fish between two plates. Sprinkle with pepper.

4. Place one bagel half on each plate and serve.

Nutrition Facts:
Bran Cereal

Exchanges/Choices
2 Starch
1/2 Fat-Free Milk

Calories	167
Calories from Fat	12
Total Fat	**1 g**
Saturated Fat	0 g
Cholesterol	**2 mg**
Sodium	**363 mg**
Carbohydrate	**42 g**
Dietary Fiber	18 g
Sugars	17 g
Protein	**8 g**

Bran Cereal

Preparation time: 2 minutes
Serves 2/Serving size: 1/2 recipe

- 1 cup bran cereal
- 1 cup fat-free milk

1. Pour cereal into two bowls and pour milk on top.

Toasted Turkey Breakfast Sandwich

with Bran Cereal

You can eat this 3-minute sandwich on the run! Or you can assemble it the night before and quickly toast or broil it the next morning.

Countdown

♦ Make sandwich

♦ Assemble cereal

SHOPPING LIST

PRODUCE
1 medium cucumber

DELI
1/2 lb sliced smoked turkey breast

STAPLES
Whole-wheat bread
Reduced-fat mayonnaise
Bran Cereal
Fat-free milk
Salt
Black peppercorns

Toasted Turkey Breakfast Sandwich

Preparation time: 5 minutes
Serves 2/Serving size: 1/2 recipe

- 4 slices whole-wheat bread
- 1 Tbsp reduced-fat mayonnaise
- 1/2 lb sliced smoked turkey breast
- 1 cucumber, peeled and sliced (1 cup)
  Salt and freshly ground black pepper to taste

1. Spread bread with mayonnaise. Divide turkey slices into four portions. Place one portion on each bread slice.

2. Toast in toaster oven or under broiler for 1–2 minutes.

3. Remove and place cucumber slices on top of 2 slices of bread. Sprinkle with salt and pepper and serve.

Nutrition Facts:
Toasted Turkey
Breakfast Sandwich

Exchanges/Choices
2 Starch
3 Lean Meat

Calories	314
Calories from Fat	79
Total Fat	**9 g**
Saturated Fat	2 g
Cholesterol	**64 mg**
Sodium	**1,435 mg**
Carbohydrate	**29 g**
Dietary Fiber	4 g
Sugars	5 g
Protein	**28 g**

Bran Cereal

Preparation time: 2 minutes
Serves 2/Serving size: 1/2 recipe

- 1 cup bran cereal
- 1 cup fat-free milk

1. Pour cereal into two bowls and pour milk on top.

Nutrition Facts:
Bran Cereal

Exchanges/Choices
2 Starch
1/2 Fat-Free Milk

Calories	167
Calories from Fat	12
Total Fat	**1 g**
Saturated Fat	0 g
Cholesterol	**2 mg**
Sodium	**363 mg**
Carbohydrate	**42 g**
Dietary Fiber	18 g
Sugars	17 g
Protein	**8 g**

Nutty Cinnamon French Toast

with Oatmeal

Sweet cinnamon and crunchy almonds top this easy French toast.

Countdown

♦ Make oatmeal

♦ Make French toast

SHOPPING LIST

GROCERY

1 small package slivered almonds

STAPLES

Egg substitute

Sugar

Ground cinnamon

Canola oil

Whole-wheat bread

Oatmeal

Fat-free milk

Nutrition Facts:
Nutty Cinnamon
French Toast

Exchanges/Choices
2 1/2 Starch
2 Lean Meat
2 Fat

Calories	350
Calories from Fat	136
Total Fat	15 g
Saturated Fat	1 g
Cholesterol	0 mg
Sodium	527 mg
Carbohydrate	37 g
Dietary Fiber	7 g
Sugars	8 g
Protein	20 g

Nutty Cinnamon French Toast

Preparation time: 15 minutes
Serves 2/Serving size: 2 slices

1 cup egg substitute
2 tsp sugar, divided
1 tsp cinnamon
1/4 cup slivered almonds
2 tsp canola oil
4 slices whole-wheat bread

1. Mix egg substitute and 1 tsp sugar together in a medium-size bowl. In a separate small bowl, mix 1 tsp sugar, cinnamon, and almonds.

2. Heat oil in a large nonstick skillet over medium-high heat. Dip bread in egg mixture, turning to coat both sides.

3. Cook French toast 1 minute and turn. Sprinkle cinnamon mixture on cooked side of bread.

4. Cover skillet with a lid and cook 2 minutes.

Nutrition Facts:
Oatmeal

Exchanges/Choices
1 1/2 Starch
1/2 Fat-Free Milk

Calories	150
Calories from Fat	20
Total Fat	2 g
Saturated Fat	0.4 g
Cholesterol	0 mg
Sodium	70 mg
Carbohydrate	25 g
Dietary Fiber	3 g
Sugars	6 g
Protein	9 g

Oatmeal

Preparation time: 5 minutes
Serves 2/Serving size: 1/2 cup

2/3 cup oatmeal
1 cup water
1 cup fat-free milk

1. Place oatmeal in a microwave-safe bowl and add water.

2. Microwave on high 3 minutes.

3. Place in two bowls and serve with milk.

Lunch

Salads

Sandwiches

Soups

Ham, Swiss, Apple, and Spinach Salad

Baby spinach leaves, ham, apple, and Swiss cheese make up this quick-to-fix lunch salad.

Helpful Hints

◆ Ask for ham to be cut in one piece to make into cubes.

◆ Any type of apple can be used. Golden Delicious will not turn brown quickly.

Countdown

◆ Prepare ingredients

◆ Assemble salad

SHOPPING LIST

PRODUCE
1 bag washed, ready-to-eat
    baby spinach
1 medium Golden Delicious apple
1 medium tomato

DAIRY
1 oz reduced-fat Swiss cheese

DELI
6 oz lean ham

STAPLES
Reduced-fat oil and balsamic
    vinegar salad dressing
Whole-wheat bread

Exchanges/Choices
1 Starch
1/2 Fruit
1 Vegetable
3 Lean Meat

Calories	285
Calories from Fat	65
Total Fat	**7 g**
Saturated Fat	2.2 g
Cholesterol	**45 mg**
Sodium	**1,175 mg**
Carbohydrate	**31 g**
Dietary Fiber	6 g
Sugars	15 g
Protein	**26 g**

Ham, Swiss, Apple, and Spinach Salad

Preparation time: 5 minutes
Serves: 2/Serving size: 1/2 recipe

4 cups washed, ready-to-eat baby spinach
1 Golden Delicious apple, cored and cut into slices (1 1/4-cups)
2 Tbsp reduced-fat oil and balsamic vinegar dressing
1 oz reduced-fat Swiss cheese, torn into bite-size pieces (1/4 cup)
6 oz extra-lean low-sodium ham cut into 1/2-inch cubes (about 1 1/2 cups)
1 medium tomato, cut into small wedges (3/4 to 1 cup)
2 slices whole-wheat bread (about 1 oz each)

1. Place spinach and apple in a salad bowl. Add dressing and toss well.

2. Sprinkle cheese and ham on top.

3. Arrange tomato wedges around edge.

4. Serve with whole-wheat bread.

Shrimp and Black-Eyed Pea Salad

with Peaches

In the South, black-eyed pea salad is also known as Mississippi Caviar. I've added some cooked shrimp to make this quick lunch salad a more complete meal. Black-eyed peas are a small beige bean that have a black circle at their inner curve and were originally imported for livestock feed.

Helpful Hints

◆ You can use frozen or canned black-eyed peas in this salad, but be sure to rinse the canned ones. I prefer to use frozen black-eyed peas. They have an excellent texture and flavor and work well in this recipe.

◆ Buy peeled, cooked shrimp from the seafood counter.

◆ You can use any type of lettuce.·

Countdown

◆ Cook black-eyed peas

◆ Assemble salad

◆ Prepare fruit

SHOPPING LIST
PRODUCE
1 red bell pepper
1 small head red leaf lettuce
2 medium peaches

SEAFOOD
6 oz peeled cooked shrimp

GROCERY
1 8-oz package frozen
    black-eyed peas or
      2 cans black-eyed peas

STAPLES
Red onion
Oil and balsamic vinegar dressing
Hot pepper sauce
Whole-wheat bread
Salt
Black peppercorns

Nutrition Facts:
Shrimp and
Black-Eyed Pea Salad

Exchanges/Choices
3 Starch
1 Vegetable
3 Lean Meat
1 1/2 Fat

Calories	423
Calories from Fat	100
Total Fat	11 g
Saturated Fat	2 g
Cholesterol	165 mg
Sodium	430 mg
Carbohydrate	50 g
Dietary Fiber	20 g
Sugars	7 g
Protein	32 g

Shrimp and Black-Eyed Pea Salad

Preparation time: 15 minutes
Serves 2/Serving size: 1/2 recipe

- 1 8-oz package frozen black-eyed peas (1 1/2 cups) or 1 1/2 cups canned black-eyed peas, rinsed and drained
- 2 Tbsp oil and vinegar salad dressing
- 1/2 cup diced red onion
  Several drops hot pepper sauce
  Salt and freshly ground black pepper to taste
- 1/2 cup diced red bell pepper
- 6 oz peeled cooked shrimp
  Several red leaf lettuce leaves, rinsed and dried
- 2 slices whole-wheat bread

1. Bring a medium-size saucepan half filled with water to a boil. Add the black-eyed peas, cover with a lid, and cook 15 minutes or until the peas are soft. Or, place in a microwave-safe bowl with 2 Tbsp water and microwave on high 5 minutes. (Omit this step if using canned black-eyed peas.)

2. Place dressing in a medium-size mixing bowl and add onion, hot pepper sauce, salt, and pepper.

3. Drain black-eyed peas and add to dressing with red bell pepper and shrimp. Toss well. Taste for seasoning. Add more salt, pepper, or hot pepper sauce to taste.

4. Line two dinner plates with lettuce leaves and spoon salad on top.

5. Serve with bread.

Nutrition Facts:
Peaches

Exchanges/Choices
1 Fruit

Calories	38
Calories from Fat	0
Total Fat	0.2 g
Saturated Fat	0 g
Cholesterol	0 mg
Sodium	0 mg
Carbohydrate	9 g
Dietary Fiber	1 g
Sugars	8 g
Protein	1 g

Peaches

1. Serve one medium peach per person.

Tuscan Bean and Tuna Salad with Tomatoes

with Watermelon Cubes

Vinaigrette dressing makes this popular Italian salad a nice change from tuna salad with a mayonnaise base. The tomatoes are a colorful complement.

Helpful Hints

◆ You can use any type of canned bean in this salad.

◆ Buy the best quality white meat tuna packed in water for the tastiest results.

◆ You can find watermelon cubes in season in the produce section of most supermarkets.

Countdown

◆ Make salad

SHOPPING LIST

PRODUCE
1 small bunch parsley
1 small head red leaf lettuce
2 medium tomatoes
1 small container watermelon cubes
   (about 2 cups)

GROCERY
1 6-oz can white meat tuna
   packed in water
1 8-oz can white beans
   (cannellini or navy)

STAPLES

Red onion
Oil and balsamic vinegar dressing
Salt
Black peppercorns

Nutrition Facts: Tuscan Bean and Tuna Salad with Tomatoes	
Exchanges/Choices	
1 1/2 Starch	
3 Lean Meat	
2 Vegetable	
1 Fat	
Calories	352
Calories from Fat	72
Total Fat	8 g
Saturated Fat	1 g
Cholesterol	21 mg
Sodium	612 mg
Carbohydrate	36 g
Dietary Fiber	10 g
Sugars	8 g
Protein	30 g

Tuscan Bean and Tuna Salad with Tomatoes

Preparation time: 10 minutes
Serves 2/Serving size: 1/2 recipe

  1 cup rinsed and drained small white beans (cannellini or navy)
1/4 cup diced red onion
  1 6-oz can white meat tuna packed in water
1/2 cup chopped fresh parsley, divided
  2 Tbsp plus 2 tsp oil and balsamic vinegar dressing
     Salt and freshly ground black pepper
1/2 head red leaf lettuce
  2 cups tomatoes, cut into 1/2-inch pieces

1. Place beans in a serving bowl and add onion.

2. Drain tuna and break into large flakes. Add to the beans.

3. Add half the parsley, 2 Tbsp dressing, and salt and pepper to taste. Gently toss.

4. Arrange lettuce leaves on a serving platter and spoon salad over the leaves.

5. Toss tomatoes with 2 tsp dressing, add salt and pepper to taste, and toss again.

6. Arrange tomatoes around edges of salad plate.

7. Sprinkle tuna and tomatoes with the remaining parsley and serve.

Nutrition Facts: Watermelon Cubes	
Exchanges/Choices	
1 Fruit	
Calories	46
Calories from Fat	0
Total Fat	0.2 g
Saturated Fat	0 g
Cholesterol	0 mg
Sodium	2 mg
Carbohydrate	11 g
Dietary Fiber	0 g
Sugars	9 g
Protein	1 g

Watermelon Cubes

1. Serve one cup per person.

Antipasto Platter

with Seedless Grapes

Little bites whether they're Spanish tapas, Mediterranean Mezze, or Italian Antipasto are always colorful and enticing. Here's a quick antipasto platter that can be assembled in just a few minutes. It's great for a weekend lunch or for guests.

Helpful Hints

◆ Look for low-fat meats in the deli to vary the recipe given.

◆ Pepperoncini are small, hot peppers that can be bought in a jar or can.

◆ Any type of vegetables can be added to the platter.

Countdown

◆ Preheat oven to 350°F to warm rolls

◆ Assemble platter

◆ Warm rolls

SHOPPING LIST

PRODUCE
1 head red leaf lettuce
2 cups seedless grapes

DELI
2 oz lean, low-sodium ham
2 oz roasted chicken

GROCERY
1 cup canned pepperoncini
2 cups sweet pimentos
1 can or jar marinated artichokes
1 small can or jar pitted black olives
2 whole-wheat rolls

Antipasto Platter

Preparation time: 10 minutes
Serves 2/Serving Size: 1/2 recipe

Nutrition Facts:
Antipasto Platter

Exchanges/Choices
2 Starch
3 Vegetable
1 Lean Meat
1 Fat

Calories	388
Calories from Fat	73
Total Fat	**8 g**
Saturated Fat	1.5 g
Cholesterol	**35 mg**
Sodium	**897 mg**
Carbohydrate	**60 g**
Dietary Fiber	8 g
Sugars	14 g
Protein	**21 g**

- 1/2 head red lettuce leaves (about 3 cups)
- 2 oz sliced lean low-sodium ham (about 1/2 cup)
- 2 oz roasted chicken breast slices (about 1/2 cup)
- 1 cup canned, drained pepperoncini
- 2 cups canned/jarred sweet pimentos
- 1/2 cup canned or jarred marinated artichoke quarters (6.5 oz jar), drained
- 8 pitted black olives
- 2 whole-wheat rolls (1 3/4 oz each)

1. Preheat oven or toaster oven to 300°F to warm rolls.

2. Wash and dry lettuce leaves and place on two plates.

3. Starting in the center, arrange ham slices overlapping each other in a line toward the edge of the plate. Arrange a line of chicken on opposite side of the plate.

4. Fill in the rest of the plate with the remaining vegetables and olives.

5. Warm whole-wheat rolls in oven and serve with antipasto.

Seedless Grapes

1. Serve one cup of seedless grapes per person.

Nutrition Facts:
Seedless Grapes

Exchanges/Choices
1 Fruit

Calories	58
Calories from Fat	0
Total Fat	**0 g**
Saturated Fat	0 g
Cholesterol	**0 mg**
Sodium	**0 mg**
Carbohydrate	**15 g**
Dietary Fiber	0 g
Sugars	13 g
Protein	**0 g**

Shrimp Caesar Salad

with Kiwis

Succulent shrimp and romaine lettuce are the base for this tasty Caesar salad.

Helpful Hints

◆ Buy peeled, cooked shrimp from the seafood counter.

◆ Buy good-quality Parmesan cheese and ask the market to grate it for you or chop it in the food processor. Freeze extra for quick use. You can spoon out the quantity you need and leave the rest frozen.

Countdown

◆ Warm bread

◆ Assemble salad

◆ Prepare fruit

SHOPPING LIST

PRODUCE
1 bag washed ready-to-eat
    Romaine lettuce
2 medium Kiwis

SEAFOOD
6 oz peeled and cooked
    medium shrimp

GROCERY
2 whole-wheat pita breads
1 bottle Caesar dressing

STAPLES
Parmesan cheese
Black peppercorns

Shrimp Caesar Salad

Preparation time: 5 minutes
Serves 2/Serving size: 1/2 recipe

- 4 cups washed ready-to-eat Romaine lettuce
- 6 oz peeled and cooked medium shrimp
- 2 Tbsp Caesar salad dressing
- 2 whole-wheat pita breads
- 2 Tbsp grated Parmesan cheese
  Freshly ground black pepper to taste

1. Preheat oven or toaster oven to 300°F.

2. Place lettuce and shrimp in a bowl and toss with dressing. Place pita bread in oven.

3. Divide salad between two plates. Sprinkle Parmesan on top and add pepper.

4. Serve with warm whole-wheat pita bread.

Nutrition Facts:
Shrimp Caesar Salad

Exchanges/Choices
2 Starch
3 Lean Meat
1 1/2 Fat

Calories	337
Calories from Fat	106
Total Fat	12 g
Saturated Fat	2 g
Cholesterol	172 mg
Sodium	517 mg
Carbohydrate	33 g
Dietary Fiber	2 g
Sugars	4 g
Protein	27 g

Kiwis

1. Serve one kiwi per person.

Nutrition Facts:
Kiwis

Exchanges/Choices
1 Fruit

Calories	45
Calories from Fat	0
Total Fat	0 g
Saturated Fat	0 g
Cholesterol	0 mg
Sodium	0 mg
Carbohydrate	11 g
Dietary Fiber	2 g
Sugars	7 g
Protein	1 g

Smoked Fish Salad

with Fruit Yogurt

Smoked fish, onion, and dill pickles are a typical English pub lunch. I have combined these ingredients into a quick and tasty lunch salad.

Helpful Hints

◆ Choose any type of smoked white fish (haddock, amberjack, kingfish, or mackerel).

◆ To cut onion rings, slice the onion parallel to the root in 1/2-inch slices.

Countdown

◆ Blanch onion rings

◆ Assemble salad

◆ Make toast

SHOPPING LIST

PRODUCE
1 medium onion

DAIRY
2 6-oz cartons fat-free
    artificially sweetened
    fruit-flavored yogurt

DELI
1/2 lb smoked white fish

GROCERY
1 small jar dill pickles
1 small loaf rye bread

STAPLES
oil and vinegar salad dressing

Smoked Fish Salad

Preparation time: 10 minutes
Serves 2/Serving size: 1/2 recipe

Nutrition Facts:
Smoked Fish Salad

Exchanges/Choices
2 Starch
1 Vegetable
3 Lean Meat
2 Fat

Calories	379
Calories from Fat	99
Total Fat	11 g
Saturated Fat	2 g
Cholesterol	87 mg
Sodium	1,655 mg
Carbohydrate	34 g
Dietary Fiber	5 g
Sugars	8 g
Protein	34 g

    1   medium onion, sliced into rings (1 cup)
 1/2 lb smoked white fish, all bones removed
    2   Tbsp oil and vinegar salad dressing
 1/2 cup sliced dill pickles
    4   slices rye bread

1. Bring a small saucepan half filled with water to a boil. Add sliced onion rings. When water returns to a boil, drain and run rings under cold water.

2. Cut fish into pieces about 2 inches long and 1 inch wide. Place smoked fish in a shallow dish or bowl and spread onion rings on top.

3. Spoon dressing over fish and onion rings.

4. Slice pickles on the diagonal and arrange around edge of plate.

5. Toast bread and serve with salad.

Fruit Yogurt

1. Serve one cup fat-free artificially sweetened fruit-flavored yogurt per person.

Nutrition Facts:
Fruit Yogurt

Exchanges/Choices
1/2 Fat-Free Milk
1/2 Carbohydrate

Calories	70
Calories from Fat	0
Total Fat	1 g
Saturated Fat	0 g
Cholesterol	3 mg
Sodium	95 mg
Carbohydrate	11 g
Dietary Fiber	0 g
Sugars	11 g
Protein	5 g

Smoked Turkey Waldorf Salad

with Tangerines

Crunchy apples, celery, and walnuts mixed with smoked turkey make a crisp lunch salad.

Helpful Hints

- Look for smoked turkey breast in the deli department. Ask for the turkey to be cut in one thick slice so that you can make into cubes.

- If you prefer, you can use smoked chicken breast or roast chicken.

Countdown

- Make salad
- Toast bread

SHOPPING LIST

PRODUCE
1 small head Romaine lettuce
2 small red apples
2 medium tangerines

DELI
1/2 lb smoked turkey breast

GROCERY
1 small package broken walnuts

STAPLES
Reduced-fat mayonnaise
Lemon
Whole-wheat bread
Salt
Black peppercorns
Celery

Nutrition Facts:
Smoked Turkey
Waldorf Salad

Exchanges/Choices
1 Starch
1 1/2 Fruit
3 Lean Meat
1 1/2 Fat

Calories	354
Calories from Fat	88
Total Fat	10 g
Saturated Fat	2 g
Cholesterol	65 mg
Sodium	1,427 mg
Carbohydrate	40 g
Dietary Fiber	7 g
Sugars	20 g
Protein	27 g

Smoked Turkey Waldorf Salad

Preparation time: 10 minutes
Serves 2/Serving size: 1/2 recipe

2 Tbsp reduced-fat mayonnaise
2 Tbsp lemon juice
   Salt and freshly ground black pepper to taste
2 celery stalks, sliced (1 cup)
2 small red apples, cored and cut into 1/2-inch cubes (2 cups)
1 Tbsp broken walnuts (1/4 oz)
1/2 lb smoked turkey breast cut into 1/2-inch cubes
   Several romaine lettuce leaves, washed and dried
2 slices whole-wheat bread

1. Mix mayonnaise and lemon juice together in a medium-size bowl. Add salt and pepper.

2. Toss celery, apples, walnuts, and turkey in the mayonnaise. Taste for seasoning and add more salt and pepper, if needed.

3. Place lettuce leaves on two dinner plates and spoon salad onto leaves.

4. Toast whole-wheat bread and serve with salad.

Nutrition Facts:
Tangerine

Exchanges/Choices
1 Fruit

Calories	60
Calories from Fat	0
Total Fat	0 g
Saturated Fat	0 g
Cholesterol	0 mg
Sodium	0 mg
Carbohydrate	15 g
Dietary Fiber	2 g
Sugars	12 g
Protein	1 g

Tangerines

1. Serve one medium tangerine per person.

Italian Peasant Salad

with Plums

This colorful array of vegetables—blanched, dressed, and topped with coarsely chopped eggs—is a tasty salad served in Northern Italy. The vegetables are cooked separately in a microwave oven.

Helpful Hints

◆ Buy peeled baby carrots—they're so easy to use.

◆ You can serve the vegetables raw instead of cooked.

◆ You can use any type of lettuce.

◆ You can cook the eggs in advance and keep them several days in the refrigerator.

Countdown

◆ Cook eggs

◆ Cook vegetables

◆ Assemble salad

SHOPPING LIST

PRODUCE
1/2 lb green beans
1/2 lb peeled baby carrots
1/4 lb broccoli
1 small head Boston lettuce
1 small bunch arugula
2 medium plums

STAPLES
Eggs (6 needed)
Whole-wheat bread
Oil and vinegar salad dressing

Nutrition Facts:
Italian Peasant Salad

Exchanges/Choices
1 Starch
3 Vegetable
2 Medium-Fat Meat

Calories	332
Calories from Fat 104	
Total Fat	12 g
Saturated Fat	2.4 g
Cholesterol	213 mg
Sodium	563 mg
Carbohydrate	40 g
Dietary Fiber	11 g
Sugars	13 g
Protein	21 g

Italian Peasant Salad

Preparation time: 15 minutes
Serves 2/Serving size: 1/2 recipe

      6 eggs
  1/2 lb green beans, trimmed (2 cups)
  1/2 lb peeled baby carrots (2 cups)
  1/4 lb broccoli florets (2 cups)
      2 Tbsp oil and vinegar salad dressing, divided
          Several leaves Boston lettuce
  1/2 cup arugula, torn into small bite-sized pieces
      2 slices whole-wheat bread

1. Place eggs in a small saucepan and cover with cold water. Place over medium-high heat and bring to a boil. Reduce heat to low and gently simmer 12 minutes.

2. Drain and fill the pan with cold water. When eggs are cool to the touch, peel and cut in half lengthwise. Remove the yolks from four of the eggs and discard.

3. Coarsely chop the six egg whites and two yolks. Set aside.

4. Place beans, carrots, and broccoli in three separate bowls. Cook each vegetable in a microwave oven on high for 2 minutes.

5. Place vegetables in a medium-size mixing bowl and toss with 1 Tbsp dressing.

6. Place lettuce leaves on two plates and arrange vegetables in the center.

7. Sprinkle coarsely chopped eggs on top of the vegetables, sprinkle with arugula, and drizzle remaining dressing over the salad.

8. Serve with whole-wheat bread or toast.

Nutrition Facts:
Plum

Exchanges/Choices
1/2 Fruit

Calories	30
Calories from Fat	0
Total Fat	0 g
Saturated Fat	0 g
Cholesterol	0 mg
Sodium	0 mg
Carbohydrate	8 g
Dietary Fiber	1 g
Sugars	7 g
Protein	0 g

Plums

1. Serve one medium plum per person.

Toasted Almond Chicken Salad

with Pineapple Chunks

Chicken salad is easy to make using ready-to-eat cooked chicken pieces.

Helpful Hints

◆ Look for ready-to-eat roasted chicken strips in the cooked meat section or in the refrigerated ready-to-eat meat cases of the supermarket.

◆ If you do not have a toaster oven, toast almonds in a small skillet over medium heat for about 30 seconds or until golden.

◆ You can find fresh pineapple chunks in the produce section of the supermarket.

Countdown

◆ Make salad

SHOPPING LIST

PRODUCE
1 package fresh pineapple chunks

MEAT
1/2 lb ready-to-eat roasted chicken
    strips

GROCERY
1 small package sliced almonds
1 small loaf rye bread
1 bottle dried dill

STAPLES
Reduced-fat mayonnaise
Celery
Salt
Black peppercorns

Toasted Almond Chicken Salad

Preparation time: 5 minutes
Serves 2/Serving size: 1/2 recipe

- 8 oz ready-to-eat roasted chicken strips
- 2 stalks celery, sliced (2 cups)
- 1 Tbsp slivered almonds
- 2 Tbsp reduced-fat mayonnaise
- 1 tsp dried dill
  Salt and freshly ground black pepper to taste
- 2 large slices rye bread

1. Coarsely chop chicken and celery in a food processor or by hand. Remove to a bowl.

2. Toast almonds in a toaster oven until golden.

3. Add almonds to chicken and stir in mayonnaise, dill, salt, and pepper.

4. Spoon salad onto two plates and serve with rye bread or toast.

Nutrition Facts:
Toasted Almond Chicken Salad

Exchanges/Choices
1 Starch
1 Vegetable
5 Lean Meat
1/2 Fat

Calories	365
Calories from Fat	111
Total Fat	12 g
Saturated Fat	2.3 g
Cholesterol	101 mg
Sodium	524 mg
Carbohydrate	22 g
Dietary Fiber	5 g
Sugars	2 g
Protein	40 g

Pineapple Chunks

1. Serve one cup per person.

Nutrition Facts:
Pineapple Chunks

Exchanges/Choices
1 1/2 Fruit

Calories	75
Calories from Fat	0
Total Fat	0 g
Saturated Fat	0 g
Cholesterol	0 mg
Sodium	0 mg
Carbohydrate	20 g
Dietary Fiber	2 g
Sugars	14 g
Protein	1 g

Salsa Beef Salad

with Oranges

Roast beef, salsa, shredded lettuce, and cheese give this salad the earthy flavors of the Southwest.

Helpful Hints

◆ Washed, ready-to-eat shredded lettuce is available in the produce department.

◆ Buy salsa that has no added sugar or oil.

◆ Ask for lean roast beef in the deli section of the supermarket.

Countdown

◆ Prepare ingredients

◆ Assemble salad

SHOPPING LIST

PRODUCE
1 bag washed, ready-to-eat
 shredded lettuce
1 orange

DAIRY
1 small package shredded, reduced-
 fat Monterey Jack cheese

DELI
6 oz sliced, lean roast beef

GROCERY
1 small jar tomato salsa
2 seven-grain dinner rolls
1 small package frozen corn kernels
1 small can red kidney beans

STAPLES
Reduced-fat oil and vinegar
 dressing

Nutrition Facts:
Salsa Beef Salad

Exchanges/Choices
3 1/2 Starch
1 Vegetable
2 Lean Meat
1/2 Fat

Calories	410
Calories from Fat	70
Total Fat	8 g
Saturated Fat	1.7 g
Cholesterol	35 mg
Sodium	1,000 mg
Carbohydrate	57 g
Dietary Fiber	11 g
Sugars	9 g
Protein	29 g

Salsa Beef Salad

Preparation time: 5 minutes
Serves: 2/Serving size: 1/2 recipe

- 4 oz sliced deli lean roast beef
- 5 cups shredded lettuce
- 1/4 cup tomato salsa
- 2 Tbsp reduced-fat oil and vinegar dressing
- 1/2 cup frozen corn kernels
- 1 cup rinsed, drained canned red kidney beans
- 2 medium seven-grain rolls (about 1 3/4 oz each)

1. Preheat oven or toaster oven to 300°F.

2. Slice beef into 2-inch strips.

3. Arrange lettuce on a serving platter and place beef strips on top.

4. Mix salsa with oil and vinegar dressing and spoon over salad.

5. Defrost corn in microwave oven on high 1 minute.

6. Sprinkle red kidney beans and corn on top.

7. Serve with seven-grain rolls.

Nutrition Facts:
Orange

Exchanges/Choices
1 Fruit

Calories	70
Calories from Fat	0
Total Fat	0 g
Saturated Fat	0 g
Cholesterol	0 mg
Sodium	0 mg
Carbohydrate	18 g
Dietary Fiber	4 g
Sugars	14 g
Protein	1 g

Orange
1. Peel orange and divide between two small dessert plates.

Chef's Salad
with Apples

A salad of julienne slices of turkey, ham, cheese, and vegetables served on a crisp bed of lettuce and topped with dressing has been an American staple for nearly 100 years. Over the years, the ingredients have changed, but the style of assorted meats, cheese, and vegetables remains the same. Here is a simple, quick version.

Helpful Hints

◆ The vegetables can be cut in a food processor using a julienne blade or simply slice the vegetables using the slicing blade.

◆ Buy turkey and ham that are not honey baked and do not have added sugar.

Countdown

◆ Prepare ingredients

◆ Assemble salad

SHOPPING LIST
PRODUCE
1 bag washed, ready-to-eat lettuce
1 medium cucumber
1 small green bell pepper
1 medium tomato
2 small apples

DELI
3 oz smoked turkey breast
2 oz lean, low-sodium ham

DAIRY
1 oz reduced-fat cheddar cheese

STAPLES
Reduced-fat oil and vinegar
    dressing
Whole-wheat bread

Nutrition Facts:
Chef's Salad

Exchanges/Choices
1 Starch
2 Vegetable
2 Lean Meat
1 Fat

Calories	265
Calories from Fat	70
Total Fat	8 g
Saturated Fat	2.7 g
Cholesterol	45 mg
Sodium	1,050 mg
Carbohydrate	27 g
Dietary Fiber	6 g
Sugars	11 g
Protein	23 g

Chef's Salad

Preparation time: 5 minutes
Serves: 2/Serving size: 1/2 recipe

4 cups washed, ready-to-eat lettuce
3 oz smoked turkey breast, cut in julienne slices (3/4 cup)
2 oz lean low-sodium ham, cut in julienne slices (1/2 cup)
1 oz reduced-fat cheddar cheese, cut in julienne slices (1/4 cup)
1/2 cucumber, peeled and cut in julienne slices (1 1/4 cup)
1 small green bell pepper, seeded and cut in julienne slices (2 cups)
1 medium tomato, quartered
2 Tbsp reduced-fat oil and vinegar dressing
2 slices whole-wheat bread (about 1 oz each)

1. Place the lettuce on a platter.

2. Arrange the turkey, ham, cheese, cucumber, green pepper, and tomato in pie-shaped wedges over the lettuce.

3. Drizzle dressing over vegetables.

4. Serve with whole-wheat bread.

Nutrition Facts:
Small Apple

Exchanges/Choices
1 Fruit

Calories	55
Calories from Fat	0
Total Fat	0 g
Saturated Fat	0 g
Cholesterol	0 mg
Sodium	0 mg
Carbohydrate	14 g
Dietary Fiber	2 g
Sugars	11 g
Protein	0 g

Apples

1. Serve one apple per person for dessert.

Tangy Chicken and Pear Salad

with Fresh Blueberries

Chicken and sweet juicy pears blend with spicy horseradish to make a tangy lunch salad.

Countdown

◆ Prepare ingredients

◆ Assemble salad

◆ Toast bread

SHOPPING LIST

PRODUCE
1 lime or lemon
1 small head Romaine lettuce
1 ripe pear
1 small bunch chives
1/2 pint fresh blueberries

DELI
1/2 lb roasted chicken breast

GROCERY
1 small jar horseradish

STAPLES
Reduced-fat mayonnaise
Dijon mustard
Whole-wheat bread

Nutrition Facts:
Tangy Chicken and
Pear Salad

Exchanges/Choices
1 Starch
1 Fruit
5 Lean Meat
1/2 Fat

Calories	390
Calories from Fat	102
Total Fat	11 g
Saturated Fat	2 g
Cholesterol	101 mg
Sodium	764 mg
Carbohydrate	32 g
Dietary Fiber	5 g
Sugars	15 g
Protein	41 g

Tangy Chicken and Pear Salad

Preparation time: 5 minutes
Serves 2/Serving size: 1/2 recipe

2 Tbsp reduced-fat mayonnaise
2 Tbsp horseradish
2 Tbsp Dijon mustard
1 Tbsp lime or lemon juice
1 ripe pear, cored and cut into 1/2-inch pieces
1/2 lb roasted boneless skinless rotisserie chicken breast, cubed
8 Romaine lettuce leaves, washed
4 Tbsp chopped fresh chives
2 slices whole-wheat bread

1. Mix mayonnaise, horseradish, mustard, and lime or lemon juice together in a salad bowl. Add pear and chicken.

2. Place lettuce leaves on two plates. Spoon salad on top and sprinkle chives on salad.

3. Toast whole-wheat bread and serve with salad.

Nutrition Facts:
Blueberries

Exchanges/Choices
1 1/2 Fruit

Calories	85
Calories from Fat	0
Total Fat	0 g
Saturated Fat	0 g
Cholesterol	0 mg
Sodium	0 mg
Carbohydrate	21 g
Dietary Fiber	3 g
Sugars	14 g
Protein	1 g

Fresh Blueberries
1. Serve one cup per person.

Italian Hero Sandwich

with Grapefruit

Heros, submarines, hoagies—call them what you like. These American sandwiches are bigger than life. This one is easy to make and doesn't break the carbohydrate budget.

Helpful Hints

◆ Any type of lean deli meat can be used.

◆ Fresh arugula and basil can be added.

Countdown

◆ Prepare ingredients

◆ Assemble sandwich

SHOPPING LIST

PRODUCE
2 plum tomatoes
1 grapefruit

DELI
4 oz roasted chicken breast

GROCERY
2 small French or Italian whole-
　grain rolls, about 2 oz each
1 small jar/can pimentos
1 small jar/can black pitted olives

STAPLES
Olive oil spray
Salt
Black peppercorns

Nutrition Facts:
Italian Hero Sandwich

Exchanges/Choices
2 Starch
1 Vegetable
2 Lean Meat

Calories	309
Calories from Fat	56
Total Fat	6 g
Saturated Fat	1.3 g
Cholesterol	50 mg
Sodium	455 mg
Carbohydrate	41 g
Dietary Fiber	6 g
Sugars	16 g
Protein	22 g

Italian Hero Sandwich

Preparation time: 5 minutes
Serves: 2/Serving size: 1/2 recipe

2 small French or Italian whole-grain rolls, (2 oz each)
    Olive oil spray
2 plum tomatoes, thinly sliced
4 oz roasted chicken pieces (1 cup)
8 pitted black olives, cut in half
1 cup drained, canned pimentos, cut into strips
    Salt and freshly ground black pepper

1. Slice rolls in half horizontally and remove the centers. Spray each side with olive oil.

2. Layer the tomato and chicken on one side of the roll. Add the olives, pimentos, salt, and pepper to taste.

3. Cover with top of roll, cut in half, and serve.

Nutrition Facts:
Grapefruit

Exchanges/Choices
1/2 Fruit

Calories	39
Calories from Fat	0
Total Fat	0 g
Saturated Fat	0 g
Cholesterol	0 mg
Sodium	0 mg
Carbohydrate	21 g
Dietary Fiber	1 g
Sugars	9 g
Protein	1 g

Grapefruit

1. Cut grapefruit in half and run knife around edge and between segments. Serve 1/2 per person.

Grilled Turkey Sausage with Mustard and Sweet Pickle Relish

with Fresh Strawberries

Grilled turkey sausages with mustard and pickle relish make a delicious change from traditional hot dogs. There are several different flavors of low-fat turkey sausages available. They come spicy or mild, smoked or plain. Pick your favorite for this tasty lunch.

Helpful Hints

♦ If you can't find whole-wheat hot dog buns, use two slices of whole-wheat bread instead.

♦ If you don't have a stovetop grill, you can use a sauté pan or a broiler.

Countdown

♦ Cook sausages

♦ Assemble sandwich

SHOPPING LIST

PRODUCE
2 medium tomatoes
1 pint fresh strawberries

MEAT
1 small package low-fat turkey sausage

GROCERY
1 jar sweet pickle relish
1 package whole-wheat hot dog buns

STAPLES
Mustard
Olive oil cooking spray

Nutrition Facts:
Grilled Turkey Sausage
with Mustard and Sweet
Pickle Relish

Exchanges/Choices
1 1/2 Starch
1 Carbohydrate
1 Vegetable
2 Lean Meat
1/2 Fat

Calories	329
Calories from Fat 107	
Total Fat	12 g
Saturated Fat	3 g
Cholesterol	72 mg
Sodium	2,166 mg
Carbohydrate	37 g
Dietary Fiber	7 g
Sugars	15 g
Protein	22 g

Grilled Turkey Sausage with Mustard and Sweet Pickle Relish

Preparation time: 15 minutes
Serves 2/Serving size: 1/2 recipe

Olive oil cooking spray
2 low-fat turkey sausages (1/2 pound)
2 whole-wheat hot dog buns
1 Tbsp mustard
2 Tbsp sweet pickle relish
2 medium tomatoes, sliced

1. Heat a stovetop grill over medium-high heat. Spray grill with cooking spray. Grill sausages 8–10 minutes, turning to make sure all sides are cooked.

2. While sausages cook, open hot dog buns and toast on grill for 2 minutes.

3. Spread mustard on buns. Add sausage and spoon relish on top.

4. Serve sliced tomatoes on the side.

Nutrition Facts:
Strawberries

Exchanges/Choices
1 Fruit

Calories	45
Calories from Fat	5
Total Fat	0.5 g
Saturated Fat	0 g
Cholesterol	0 mg
Sodium	0 mg
Carbohydrate	11 g
Dietary Fiber	4 g
Sugars	7 g
Protein	1 g

Fresh Strawberries

1. Serve one cup per person.

Shrimp Roll
with Apples

Shrimp tossed with homemade tartar sauce is a New England favorite. Drive along the coastline from Connecticut to Maine and you'll find little roadside stands selling lobster, shrimp, or clam rolls. This simple version captures their flavor.

Helpful Hints

◆ Buy peeled, cooked shrimp from the seafood counter.

◆ If whole-wheat hot dog buns are not available, use two slices of whole-wheat bread.

Countdown

◆ Make filling

◆ Assemble sandwich

SHOPPING LIST

PRODUCE
1 head lettuce or 1 bag washed
    shredded ready-to-eat lettuce
2 medium apples

SEAFOOD
6 oz peeled cooked shrimp

GROCERY
1 jar sweet pickle relish
2 whole-wheat hot dog buns

STAPLES
Reduced-fat mayonnaise
Dijon mustard
Salt
Black peppercorns

Shrimp Roll

Preparation time: 5 minutes
Serves 2/Serving size: 1/2 recipe

Nutrition Facts:
Shrimp Roll

Exchanges/Choices
2 Starch
3 Lean Meat
1 1/2 Fat

Calories	319
Calories from Fat	121
Total Fat	13 g
Saturated Fat	2 g
Cholesterol	229 mg
Sodium	689 mg
Carbohydrate	24 g
Dietary Fiber	6 g
Sugars	4 g
Protein	29 g

> 2 Tbsp reduced-fat mayonnaise
> 1 tsp Dijon mustard
> 1 Tbsp drained sweet pickle relish
>   Salt and freshly ground black pepper to taste
> 1/2 lb peeled cooked shrimp
> 2 whole-wheat hot dog buns
> 1 cup washed shredded lettuce

1. Mix mayonnaise, mustard, and relish together in a medium bowl. Add salt and pepper.

2. Add shrimp and toss to coat.

3. Split hot dog rolls open and toast in a toaster oven or under a broiler.

4. Fill rolls with lettuce and shrimp mixture.

Apples

1. Serve one medium apple per person.

Nutrition Facts:
Medium Apple

Exchanges/Choices
1 1/2 Fruit

Calories	72
Calories from Fat	0
Total Fat	0 g
Saturated Fat	0 g
Cholesterol	0 mg
Sodium	1 mg
Carbohydrate	19 g
Dietary Fiber	3 g
Sugars	14 g
Protein	0 g

Quick Turkey Wrap
with Tangerines

Turkey slices, sweet pimientos, and pickles rolled together in a soft tortilla make a colorful, quick sandwich that can be eaten on the run.

Helpful Hint

◆ This filling's also great in a whole-wheat pita pocket.

Countdown

◆ Prepare ingredients

◆ Assemble wrap

SHOPPING LIST

PRODUCE
4 tangerines

DELI
1/2 lb sliced turkey breast

GROCERY
1 small jar sliced sweet pimentos
1 jar sliced dill pickles
1 package 8-inch flour tortillas

STAPLES
Reduced-fat mayonnaise

Nutrition Facts:
Quick Turkey Wrap

Exchanges/Choices
2 Starch
1 Vegetable
4 Lean Meat

Calories	392
Calories from Fat	85
Total Fat	9 g
Saturated Fat	2 g
Cholesterol	97 mg
Sodium	927 mg
Carbohydrate	35 g
Dietary Fiber	4 g
Sugars	3 g
Protein	39 g

Quick Turkey Wrap

Preparation time: 5 minutes
Serves 2/Serving size: 1/2 recipe

> 2 8-inch flour tortillas
> 2 Tbsp reduced-fat mayonnaise
> 1/2 lb sliced turkey breast
> 1 cup sliced sweet pimentos
> 1/2 cup sliced dill pickles

1. Place tortillas on the countertop and spread with mayonnaise. Arrange turkey slices on top.

2. Spoon 1/2 cup sweet pimentos on each wrap.

3. Place 1/4 cup dill pickles on each wrap.

4. Roll wrap, slice in half, and serve. If not serving immediately, roll wrap in foil or plastic wrap to keep it from drying out.

Nutrition Facts:
Tangerines

Exchanges/Choices
2 Fruit

Calories	115
Calories from Fat	5
Total Fat	0.5 g
Saturated Fat	0.1 g
Cholesterol	0 mg
Sodium	0 mg
Carbohydrate	29 g
Dietary Fiber	4 g
Sugars	23 g
Protein	2 g

Tangerines

1. Serve two tangerines per person.

Chicken Avocado Wrap
with Oranges

Ripe avocado mixed with tomatoes, onion, and hot pepper sauce makes a tasty, quick filling for colorful tortilla wraps.

Helpful Hints

◆ Some supermarkets carry flavored, colorful tortillas—look for them!

◆ To help avocados ripen, remove the stem and place them in a bag in a warm spot.

◆ Choose plain roasted chicken strips or pieces instead of honey-baked, barbecued, or flavored with sugary coatings.

◆ Using frozen chopped onion is a great timesaver—keep a bag on hand.

Countdown

◆ Make filling

◆ Assemble wrap

SHOPPING LIST
PRODUCE
1 small onion
1 small avocado
1 medium tomato
1 lemon or lime
2 medium oranges

MEAT
6 oz roasted chicken breast

GROCERY
1 package 8-inch flour tortillas
1 small package pine nuts

STAPLES
Hot pepper sauce
Salt
Black peppercorns

Nutrition Facts:
Chicken Avocado Wrap

Exchanges/Choices
2 Starch
1 Vegetable
3 Lean Meat
3 Fat

Calories	423
Calories from Fat	146
Total Fat	16 g
Saturated Fat	4 g
Cholesterol	72 mg
Sodium	309 mg
Carbohydrate	35 g
Dietary Fiber	5 g
Sugars	4 g
Protein	34 g

Chicken Avocado Wrap

Preparation time: 10 minutes
Serves 2/Serving size: 1/2 recipe

1/4 peeled onion or 2 Tbsp frozen chopped onion
1 medium tomato, quartered (about 3/4 cup)
1/2 ripe avocado, peeled and seed removed (about 1/2 cup)
1/2 Tbsp lemon or lime juice
Several drops hot pepper sauce
Salt and freshly ground black pepper to taste
2 8-inch flour tortillas
2 Tbsp pine nuts
6 oz roasted boneless skinless chicken breast, cut into strips about 2 inches long and 1/4-inch wide, or roasted ready-to-eat chicken strips (1 1/2 cups)

1. Chop fresh onion in a food processor or add frozen onion. Add tomato, avocado, lemon juice, hot pepper sauce, salt, and pepper. Process to coarsely chop, leaving chunks of avocado.

2. Spread mixture on the two tortillas and sprinkle pine nuts and chicken pieces on top.

3. Roll up each tortilla, cut in half, and serve. If not serving immediately, roll wrap in foil to keep it from drying out.

Nutrition Facts:
Orange

Exchanges/Choices
1 Fruit

Calories	70
Calories from Fat	0
Total Fat	0 g
Saturated Fat	0 g
Cholesterol	0 mg
Sodium	0 mg
Carbohydrate	18 g
Dietary Fiber	4 g
Sugars	14 g
Protein	1 g

Oranges

1. Serve one medium orange per person.

Mediterranean Egg Salad Sandwich

with Pears

Olives and red peppers are ingredients associated with the sunny Mediterranean countries. They add zing to this quick egg salad.

Helpful Hints

◆ Bought egg salad can be used. Add the capers and olives and use these proportions as a guide.

◆ The egg salad can be made in a food processor. Be careful to pulse the blades just a few times to keep it from becoming too finely chopped or mushy.

◆ Keep hard cooked eggs in the refrigerator for snacks or quick salads.

Countdown

◆ Make hard cooked eggs

◆ While eggs cook, prepare other ingredients

◆ Make egg salad

◆ Assemble sandwich

SHOPPING LIST
PRODUCE
2 medium pears

DAIRY
6 eggs

GROCERY
1 small can/jar sweet pimentos
1 small can/jar pitted green olives

STAPLES
Reduced-fat mayonnaise
Dijon mustard
Whole-wheat bread
Salt
Black peppercorns

Nutrition Facts:
Mediterranean Egg Salad
Sandwich

Exchanges/Choices
2 Starch
1 Vegetable
2 Lean Meat
1/2 Fat

Calories	325
Calories from Fat	90
Total Fat	10 g
Saturated Fat	2.2 g
Cholesterol	210 mg
Sodium	1,245 mg
Carbohydrate	36 g
Dietary Fiber	6 g
Sugars	9 g
Protein	22 g

Mediterranean Egg Salad Sandwich

Preparation time: 15 minutes
Serves: 2/Serving size: 1/2 recipe

6 eggs (hard cook 6 eggs; discard 4 of the yolks for the salad)
4 Tbsp reduced-fat mayonnaise
1 Tbsp Dijon mustard
2 Tbsp water
8 pitted large green olives, coarsely chopped
Salt and freshly ground black pepper
4 slices whole-wheat bread
1 cup sweet pimentos, cut into 2-inch strips

1. Place the eggs in a medium-size saucepan and cover with cold water. Bring the water to a simmer over medium-high heat. Reduce heat to medium low and simmer, gently, 10 minutes. Drain and fill the pan with cold water.

2. Peel eggs, cut in half, and discard 4 yolks. Mash the remaining 2 whole eggs and 6 egg whites in the same bowl.

3. Whisk together mayonnaise, mustard, water, and olives in a bowl. Add the mashed eggs and season with salt and pepper to taste. Mix well.

4. Spread the egg salad on whole-wheat bread slices. Place pimentos on top. Serve as open sandwiches.

Nutrition Facts:
Pear

Exchanges/Choices
1 1/2 Fruit

Calories	95
Calories from Fat	0
Total Fat	0 g
Saturated Fat	0 g
Cholesterol	0 mg
Sodium	0 mg
Carbohydrate	26 g
Dietary Fiber	5 g
Sugars	15 g
Protein	1 g

Pears

1. Serve one pear per person.

Steak and Portobello Mushroom Sandwich

with Sliced Mango

Steak, meaty portobello mushrooms, and sweet onions make a great sandwich. Grill or broil this steak for a leisurely weekend lunch. It tastes best warm or at room temperature.

Helpful Hints

◆ You can use skirt, strip, sirloin, or another quick-cooking steak in this recipe.

◆ If Vidalia onions are not available, use a sweet onion such as Texas Sweet, 1040, or a red onion.

Countdown

◆ Prepare ingredients

◆ Toast bread

◆ Assemble sandwich

SHOPPING LIST

PRODUCE
3 oz portobello mushrooms
1 Vidalia onion
1 medium mango

MEAT
6 oz flank steak

STAPLES
Garlic
Balsamic vinegar
Olive oil cooking spray
Whole-wheat bread
Salt
Black peppercorns

Nutrition Facts:
Steak and Portobello
Mushroom Sandwich

Exchanges/Choices
2 Starch
2 Vegetable
2 Lean Meat
1/2 Fat

Calories	275
Calories from Fat	35
Total Fat	4 g
Saturated Fat	0.8 g
Cholesterol	0 mg
Sodium	530 mg
Carbohydrate	46 g
Dietary Fiber	8 g
Sugars	6 g
Protein	15 g

Steak and Portobello Mushroom Sandwich

Preparation time: 15 minutes
Serves 2/Serving size: 1/2 recipe

   6 oz flank steak
      Salt and freshly ground black pepper to taste
1/4 cup balsamic vinegar
   4 medium cloves garlic, crushed
   1 cup sliced portobello mushrooms
   1 cup sliced Vidalia onion
   4 slices whole-wheat bread
      Olive oil cooking spray

1. Remove fat from steak. Heat a nonstick skillet over medium-high heat and add steak. Brown 2 minutes, then turn and brown 2 additional minutes. Add salt and pepper to the cooked side.

2. Mix balsamic vinegar and garlic together.

3. Remove steak to a plate and add mushrooms, onions, and vinegar mixture to the skillet. Sauté 2 minutes.

4. Return steak to skillet for 2 minutes for 1-inch thick steak, 1 minute longer for thicker steak.

5. While steak cooks, spray bread with cooking spray and toast in toaster oven or under a broiler.

6. Slice steak on the diagonal against the grain and divide between two slices of bread. Spoon the mushrooms and onions on top. Pour the pan juices over the steak. Add salt and pepper to taste. Cover with two remaining slices of bread and cut sandwich in half.

Nutrition Facts:
Mangos

Exchanges/Choices
2 Fruit

Calories	105
Calories from Fat	0
Total Fat	0 g
Saturated Fat	0 g
Cholesterol	0 mg
Sodium	0 mg
Carbohydrate	28 g
Dietary Fiber	3 g
Sugars	24 g
Protein	1 g

Sliced Mango

1. Serve one cup per person.

Crunchy Coleslaw and Turkey Sandwich

with Apples

Deli coleslaw with added tomato salsa makes a crunchy topping for this roast turkey sandwich.

Helpful Hints

◆ Look for deli coleslaw and tomato salsa that do not have added sugar.

◆ You can use any type of lean deli meat instead of turkey if you prefer.

Countdown

◆ Mix coleslaw

◆ Assemble sandwich

SHOPPING LIST

PRODUCE
2 small apples

DELI
Deli coleslaw (3 oz needed)
1/2 lb sliced roasted turkey breast

GROCERY
1 jar no-added-sugar tomato salsa

STAPLES
Whole-wheat bread
Salt
Black peppercorns

Nutrition Facts:
Crunchy Coleslaw and
Turkey Sandwich

Exchanges/Choices
2 Starch
1 Vegetable
5 Lean Meat

Calories	351
Calories from Fat	59
Total Fat	7 g
Saturated Fat	1 g
Cholesterol	94 mg
Sodium	466 mg
Carbohydrate	33 g
Dietary Fiber	5 g
Sugars	8 g
Protein	40 g

Crunchy Coleslaw and Turkey Sandwich

Preparation time: 5 minutes
Serves 2/Serving size: 1/2 recipe

1/2 cup prepared or deli coleslaw
2 Tbsp no-added-sugar tomato salsa
    Salt and freshly ground black pepper to taste
1/2 lb sliced, roasted turkey breast
4 slices whole-wheat bread

1. Drain coleslaw in a colander.

2. Toss coleslaw with tomato salsa and add salt and pepper.

3. Divide sliced turkey in half and place on two slices of bread.

4. Spoon half the coleslaw on top of the turkey and cover with remaining bread slices.

5. Serve extra coleslaw on the side.

Nutrition Facts:
Small Apple

Exchanges/Choices
1 Fruit

Calories	55
Calories from Fat	0
Total Fat	0 g
Saturated Fat	0 g
Cholesterol	0 mg
Sodium	0 mg
Carbohydrate	14 g
Dietary Fiber	2 g
Sugars	11 g
Protein	0 g

Apples

1. Serve one small apple per person.

Roast Beef Sandwich with Tomato and Corn Relish

with Fresh Strawberries

This tangy, uncooked relish and roast beef make a tasty, colorful sandwich. Most relishes need slow cooking and lots of sugar. This is a fresh relish and the corn is so sweet that no sugar is needed. It takes very little time to make.

Helpful Hint

♦ You can use parsley instead of cilantro if you prefer.

Countdown

♦ Prepare relish

♦ Assemble sandwich

SHOPPING LIST

PRODUCE
1 medium tomato
1 small red onion
1 small bunch cilantro
1 pint strawberries

DELI
6 oz sliced lean roast beef

GROCERY
1 small package frozen corn kernels

STAPLES

Balsamic vinegar
Whole-wheat bread
Salt
Black peppercorns

Nutrition Facts:
Roast Beef Sandwich with
Tomato and Corn Relish

Exchanges/Choices
2 1/2 Starch
1 Vegetable
3 Lean Meat

Calories	366
Calories from Fat	62
Total Fat	7 g
Saturated Fat	2 g
Cholesterol	54 mg
Sodium	698 mg
Carbohydrate	48 g
Dietary Fiber	7 g
Sugars	8 g
Protein	31 g

Roast Beef Sandwich with Tomato and Corn Relish

Preparation time: 10 minutes
Serves 2/Serving size: 1/2 recipe

- 1 cup frozen corn kernels
- 1 cup diced tomatoes
- 1 Tbsp balsamic vinegar
- 2 Tbsp chopped red onion
- 3 Tbsp fresh cilantro
  Salt and freshly ground black pepper to taste
- 4 slices whole-wheat bread
- 6 oz sliced lean roast beef

1. Microwave corn 30 seconds to defrost or place in boiling water for 30 seconds and drain. Mix corn with tomatoes, vinegar, onion, and cilantro. Add salt and pepper.

2. Set relish aside to marinate for a few minutes.

3. Toast bread and place roast beef on two slices.

4. Spoon relish over roast beef and cover with remaining slices of bread.

Nutrition Facts:
Strawberries

Exchanges/Choices
1 Fruit

Calories	45
Calories from Fat	5
Total Fat	0.5 g
Saturated Fat	0 g
Cholesterol	0 mg
Sodium	0 mg
Carbohydrate	11 g
Dietary Fiber	4 g
Sugars	7 g
Protein	1 g

Fresh Strawberries

1. Serve one cup per person.

Neapolitan Pizza
with Plums

Neapolitans keep their pizzas simple and tasty. This pizza is topped with fresh tomatoes, a sprinkling of garlic, Parmesan cheese, thinly sliced ham, and a touch of arugula.

Helpful Hint

◆ Buy good-quality Parmesan cheese and ask the market to grate it for you or chop it in the food processor. Freeze extra for quick use. You can spoon out the quantity you need and leave the rest frozen.

Countdown

◆ Preheat broiler

◆ Prepare ingredients

◆ Make pizza

SHOPPING LIST

PRODUCE
2 medium tomatoes
1 bunch arugula
2 medium plums

DELI
6 oz lean ham

GROCERY
1 package whole-wheat pita bread

STAPLES
Parmesan cheese
Garlic
Olive oil
Salt
Black peppercorns

Nutrition Facts:
Neapolitan Pizza

Exchanges/Choices
2 Starch
1 Vegetable
3 Lean Meat
1 Fat

Calories	373
Calories from Fat 117	
Total Fat	13 g
Saturated Fat	3 g
Cholesterol	53 mg
Sodium	1,319 mg
Carbohydrate	38 g
Dietary Fiber	4 g
Sugars	7 g
Protein	31 g

Neapolitan Pizza

Preparation time: 10 minutes
Serves 2/Serving size: 1/2 recipe

- 2 whole-wheat pita breads
- 2 medium tomatoes, diced (about 2 cups)
- 2 cloves garlic, crushed
- 2 tsp olive oil
  Salt and freshly ground black pepper to taste
- 2 Tbsp grated Parmesan cheese
- 6 oz lean ham, cut into 2-inch pieces (1 1/4 cups)
- 1/2 cup torn arugula leaves

1. Preheat broiler and line a baking sheet with foil.

2. Place pita breads on sheet and sprinkle with tomatoes, garlic, and olive oil. Add salt and pepper and sprinkle with Parmesan cheese.

3. Place under broiler 3 minutes. Add ham and return to broiler for 2 minutes.

4. Remove from boiler, sprinkle arugula on top, and serve.

Nutrition Facts:
Plum

Exchanges/Choices
1/2 Fruit

Calories	30
Calories from Fat	0
Total Fat	0 g
Saturated Fat	0 g
Cholesterol	0 mg
Sodium	0 mg
Carbohydrate	8 g
Dietary Fiber	1 g
Sugars	7 g
Protein	0 g

Plums

1. Serve one medium plum per person.

Turkey and Refried Bean Enchiladas

with Fruit Yogurt

Sliced turkey and refried beans rolled in a tortilla and topped with a spicy tomato sauce make a quick and satisfying lunch. You can put this enchilada together the night before and take it with you for lunch the next day. It will just need to be warmed in a microwave before eating.

Helpful Hints

◆ Look for no-sugar-or-oil-added tomato sauce. Any type of pasta or marinara sauce can be used.

◆ Shredded, reduced-fat Mexican style cheese can be used instead of Monterey Jack.

◆ Low-fat and no-fat refried beans can be found in the ethnic section of the supermarket.

◆ If you do not have a microwave, place enchiladas under a broiler for 5 minutes or in a toaster oven.

Countdown

◆ Prepare enchiladas

◆ Heat in microwave oven

SHOPPING LIST

DAIRY
1 small package shredded,
    reduced-fat Monterey Jack
    cheese (1 oz needed)
1 6-oz container low-fat fruit yogurt

DELI
1/4 lb sliced turkey breast

GROCERY
1 small jar low-sodium,
    no-sugar-added tomato sauce
    (8 oz needed)
1 small can low-fat or nonfat
    refried beans
1 small package 6-inch corn
    tortillas

STAPLES
Hot pepper sauce

Nutrition Facts:
Turkey and Refried Bean
Enchiladas

Exchanges/Choices
1 Starch
2 Vegetable
3 Lean Meat

Calories	335
Calories from Fat	40
Total Fat	4.5 g
Saturated Fat	2.1 g
Cholesterol	83 mg
Sodium	425 mg
Carbohydrate	35 g
Dietary Fiber	4 g
Sugars	29 g
Protein	37 g

Turkey and Refried Bean Enchiladas

Preparation time: 5 minutes
Serves: 2/Serving size: 1/2 recipe

> 2 6-inch corn tortillas
> 6 oz sliced turkey breast (about 1 to 1 1/4 cups)
> 1/4 cup canned low-fat or non-fat refried beans
> 1 cup bottled low-sodium, no-sugar-added tomato sauce
> 1/8 tsp hot pepper sauce
> 1/4 cup shredded, reduced-fat Monterey Jack cheese

1. Place tortillas on a countertop. Divide turkey slices in half and place on tortilla. Spread refried beans over the turkey.

2. Roll up tortillas and place in a microwave-safe dish just big enough to hold them, seam side down.

3. Mix tomato sauce and hot pepper sauce together and spoon over tortillas.

4. Cover with another dish or plastic wrap and microwave on high for 2 minutes. Remove cover and sprinkle with Monterey Jack cheese. Cover and microwave 1 minute. Divide between two plates and serve.

Nutrition Facts:
Fruit Yogurt

Exchanges/Choices
1/2 Fat-Free Milk
1/2 Carbohydrate

Calories	70
Calories from Fat	0
Total Fat	1 g
Saturated Fat	0 g
Cholesterol	3 mg
Sodium	95 mg
Carbohydrate	11 g
Dietary Fiber	0 g
Sugars	11 g
Protein	5 g

Fruit Yogurt

1. Divide one cup between two dessert bowls and serve.

Greek Tuna Salad Pita Pocket

with Cantaloupe

Feta cheese, olives, cucumber, and fresh greens are the base of a typical Greek salad. Add some tuna and serve in a pita pocket for a quick Greek-style lunch.

Helpful Hints

◆ Feta cheese is sheep's milk cheese and can be found in the dairy section of the supermarket.

◆ If you don't have pita bread, serve the salad over two slices of toasted whole-wheat bread as an open-faced sandwich.

◆ You can use any type of lettuce.

Countdown

◆ Prepare ingredients

◆ Assemble sandwich

SHOPPING LIST

PRODUCE
1 bag washed ready-to-eat
    Romaine lettuce
1 cucumber
1 small tomato
1 medium cantaloupe

DAIRY
1 package crumbled feta cheese

GROCERY
1 small can white meat tuna
    packed in water
1 can or jar pitted black olives
1 package whole-wheat pita bread

STAPLES
Oil and balsamic vinegar
    salad dressing

Nutrition Facts:
Greek Tuna
Salad Pita Pocket

Exchanges/Choices
2 Starch
1 Vegetable
3 Lean Meat
1 1/2 Fat

Calories	382
Calories from Fat	135
Total Fat	15 g
Saturated Fat	3 g
Cholesterol	34 mg
Sodium	781 mg
Carbohydrate	36 g
Dietary Fiber	4 g
Sugars	6 g
Protein	28 g

Greek Tuna Salad Pita Pocket

Preparation time: 5 minutes
Serves 2/Serving size: 1/2 recipe

- 1 cup washed ready-to-eat Romaine lettuce
- 1 cup cucumber pieces (1/2 inch)
- 1/2 cup tomato pieces (1/2 inch)
- 6 oz canned white meat tuna packed in water, drained and flaked (1 cup drained)
- 8 pitted black olives, cut in half
- 2 Tbsp oil and balsamic vinegar salad dressing
- 2 whole-wheat pita breads
- 1 oz crumbled feta cheese (2 Tbsp)

1. Place lettuce, cucumber, tomato, tuna, and olives in bowl and toss with dressing.

2. Cut pita bread in half and open pockets. Fill pockets with salad.

3. Sprinkle feta cheese on top.

Nutrition Facts:
Cantaloupe

Exchanges/Choices
1 Fruit

Calories	50
Calories from Fat	0
Total Fat	0 g
Saturated Fat	0 g
Cholesterol	0 mg
Sodium	10 mg
Carbohydrate	12 g
Dietary Fiber	1 g
Sugars	10 g
Protein	1 g

Cantaloupe

1. Serve 1/4 medium cantaloupe per person.

Horace's Chickpea Soup
with Apples

La Minestra di Orazio, *or Horace's Chickpea and Pasta Soup, is an ancient Roman dish. In one of his satires, Horace is quoted as saying, "I am going home to a bowl of leeks, chickpeas, and lasagna. . . ." In fact, this is one of the earliest references to pasta of any kind.*

Helpful Hints

◆ Wash leeks by cutting them in half lengthwise, then cutting each half lengthwise again and running them under cold water.

◆ Slice vegetables in a food processor fitted with a slicing blade.

Countdown

◆ Make soup

SHOPPING LIST

PRODUCE
1 leek
2 medium tomatoes
2 small apples

DELI
1/4 lb lean ham

GROCERY
1 can chickpeas (garbanzo beans)
1 small package acini pepe or
    orzo pasta

STAPLES
Celery
Parmesan cheese
Olive oil
Fat-free reduced-sodium
    chicken broth
Salt
Black peppercorns

Nutrition Facts:
Horace's Chickpea Soup

Exchanges/Choices
2 1/2 Starch
3 Vegetable
3 Lean Meat
1 1/2 Fat

Calories	453
Calories from Fat	131
Total Fat	15 g
Saturated Fat	3 g
Cholesterol	37 mg
Sodium	1,337 mg
Carbohydrate	53 g
Dietary Fiber	9 g
Sugars	11 g
Protein	30 g

Horace's Chickpea Soup

Preparation time: 20 minutes
Serves 2/Serving size: 1/2 recipe

   1 Tbsp olive oil
   2 medium stalks celery, sliced (1 cup)
   1 medium leek, sliced (1 cup)
   2 cups chopped tomatoes
 1/3 cup acini pepe or orzo pasta
 3/4 cup canned chickpeas (garbanzo beans), rinsed
        and drained
1 1/2 cups fat-free reduced-sodium chicken broth
 1/2 cup water
 1/4 lb lean ham cut into bite-sized pieces (about 1 cup)
        Salt and freshly ground black pepper to taste
   2 Tbsp freshly grated Parmesan cheese

1. Heat olive oil in a large saucepan over medium-high heat. Add celery and leeks and sauté 3 minutes.

2. Lower heat to medium and add tomatoes. Cook, covered for 5 minutes.

3. Raise heat to high and add pasta, chickpeas, chicken broth, and water. Bring to a boil and cook 8 minutes, stirring occasionally.

4. Stir in ham and add salt and pepper.

5. Serve in large soup bowls with Parmesan cheese sprinkled on top.

Nutrition Facts:
Small Apple

Exchanges/Choices
1 Fruit

Calories	55
Calories from Fat	0
Total Fat	0 g
Saturated Fat	0 g
Cholesterol	0 mg
Sodium	0 mg
Carbohydrate	14 g
Dietary Fiber	2 g
Sugars	11 g
Protein	0 g

Apples

1. Serve one small apple per person.

Sausage and Tortellini Soup

with Grapefruit

Mushroom tortellini and turkey are the base for this quick, lunch soup.

Helpful Hints

◆ Any type of lean turkey sausage can be used.

◆ Fresh or frozen mushroom tortellini can be used.

Countdown

◆ Sauté onion and garlic

◆ Complete soup

SHOPPING LIST

PRODUCE
1 small bunch fresh basil
1 grapefruit

MEAT
1/2 lb lean turkey sausage

GROCERY
1 can low-sodium, diced tomatoes
1 cup fat-free, low-sodium
    chicken broth
1 small package mushroom-stuffed
    tortellini
1 small package frozen, chopped
    onions

STAPLES
Olive oil spray
Garlic
Salt
Black peppercorns

Nutrition Facts:
Sausage and Tortellini Soup

Exchanges/Choices
1 1/2 Starch
4 Vegetable
1 Lean Meat
1/2 Fat

Calories	319
Calories from Fat	56
Total Fat	6 g
Saturated Fat	1.7 g
Cholesterol	50 mg
Sodium	1,040 mg
Carbohydrate	52 g
Dietary Fiber	8 g
Sugars	23 g
Protein	18 g

Sausage and Tortellini Soup

Preparation time: 20 minutes
Serves: 2/Serving size: 1/2 recipe

Olive oil spray
1/4 lb lean turkey sausage, cut into 1/2-inch slices
1 cup frozen, chopped onion
2 cloves garlic, crushed
2 cups drained, no added salt, diced canned tomatoes
1 cup fat-free, reduced-sodium chicken broth
1 cup water
2 oz mushroom tortellini (1 1/2 cups)
1 cup basil leaves
Salt and fresh ground pepper

1. Heat a large nonstick saucepan over medium-high heat. Spray with olive oil spray. Add turkey sausage, onion, and garlic and sauté 5 minutes.

2. Add the tomatoes, chicken broth, water, and tortellini. Bring to a low boil and cook 5 minutes or until tortellini is cooked through.

3. Remove from heat and stir in basil. Add salt and pepper to taste.

Nutrition Facts:
Grapefruit

Exchanges/Choices
1/2 Fruit

Calories	39
Calories from Fat	0
Total Fat	0 g
Saturated Fat	0 g
Cholesterol	0 mg
Sodium	0 mg
Carbohydrate	21 g
Dietary Fiber	1 g
Sugars	4 g
Protein	1 g

Grapefruit

1. Cut grapefruit in half and run knife around edge and between segments. Serve 1/2 per person.

Turkey and Vegetable Soup with Cheddar Bruschetta

with Sliced Mango

Quickly slice some vegetables, dice some leftover turkey, and you can have homemade soup in less than 20 minutes. Double the recipe and freeze the rest for another delicious meal.

Helpful Hints

◆ Use roasted turkey from the deli.

◆ Use peeled baby carrots to save time.

◆ Most ready-to-eat spinach comes in 10-oz bags. Just use half a bag for this recipe.

◆ Cut French bread on the diagonal to make long oval slices.

Countdown

◆ Prepare soup

◆ Slice fruit

◆ Make bruschetta

SHOPPING LIST

PRODUCE
1 small package peeled baby carrots
1 small package broccoli florets
1 bag washed ready-to-eat spinach
1 large mango

MEAT
6 oz roasted turkey

GROCERY
1 loaf whole-grain French bread

DAIRY
1 small package shredded
    reduced-fat cheddar cheese

STAPLES
Onion
Olive oil
Fat-free reduced-sodium
    chicken broth
Salt
Black peppercorns

Nutrition Facts:
Turkey and Vegetable
Soup with Cheddar
Bruschetta

Exchanges/Choices
1 Starch
3 Vegetable
4 Lean Meat
1/2 Fat

Calories	361
Calories from Fat	89
Total Fat	10 g
Saturated Fat	3 g
Cholesterol	79 mg
Sodium	777 mg
Carbohydrate	31 g
Dietary Fiber	2 g
Sugars	8 g
Protein	38 g

Turkey and Vegetable Soup with Cheddar Bruschetta

Preparation time: 15 minutes
Serves 2/Serving size: 1/2 recipe

2 tsp olive oil, divided
1 cup sliced onion
1 cup sliced baby carrots
2 cups broccoli florets
1 1/2 cups fat-free, reduced-sodium chicken broth
1 1/2 cups water
5 oz washed ready-to-eat spinach (about 5 cups)
6 oz roasted turkey cut into 1/2- to 1-inch pieces
(about 1 cup)
Salt and freshly ground black pepper to taste
1 oz shredded reduced-fat cheddar cheese (1/4 cup)
2 slices whole-grain French bread

1. Heat oil in a large nonstick saucepan over medium-high heat and add onion, carrots, and broccoli. Sauté 5 minutes.

2. Add chicken broth and water. Raise heat, bring to a boil, and cook 5 minutes.

3. Lower heat to medium and add spinach and turkey. Simmer 2 minutes or until turkey is warmed through and spinach is wilted.

4. Add salt and pepper.

5. Sprinkle cheddar cheese on bread slices and toast in toaster oven or under a broiler. Serve with soup.

Nutrition Facts:
Mango

Exchanges/Choices
2 Fruit

Calories	105
Calories from Fat	0
Total Fat	0 g
Saturated Fat	0 g
Cholesterol	0 mg
Sodium	0 mg
Carbohydrate	28 g
Dietary Fiber	3 g
Sugars	24 g
Protein	1 g

Sliced Mango
1. Serve one cup mango per person.

Pasta and Bean Soup
with Honeydew Melon Cubes

The addition of ham to this traditional Italian pasta and bean soup makes it hearty and perfect for lunch. You can make this 20-minute soup the night before and warm it up the next day or freeze it for later. You'll want to cook and add the pasta just before you plan to serve the soup so the pasta doesn't get mushy.

Helpful Hints

♦ You can use any type of small pasta in this soup. It's a good way to use up small quantities of pasta. They can be different shapes as long as they're roughly the same size.

♦ If soup is too thick, add more water.

♦ To quickly chop fresh basil, wash, dry, and snip the leaves with scissors right off the stem.

♦ Look for honeydew melon cubes in the produce section of most supermarkets.

Countdown

♦ Make soup

SHOPPING LIST

PRODUCE
1 small bunch basil
1 container honeydew melon cubes

DELI
1/4 lb lean ham

GROCERY
1 can cannellini beans
1 can Italian plum tomatoes
1 package small pasta

STAPLES

Celery
Parmesan cheese
Garlic
Fat-free reduced-sodium
   chicken broth
Hot pepper sauce
Olive oil
Salt
Black peppercorns

Nutrition Facts:
Pasta and Bean Soup

Exchanges/Choices
2 Starch
2 Vegetable
3 Lean Meat

Calories	361
Calories from Fat	94
Total Fat	10 g
Saturated Fat	3 g
Cholesterol	37 mg
Sodium	1,671 mg
Carbohydrate	40 g
Dietary Fiber	9 g
Sugars	8 g
Protein	30 g

Pasta and Bean Soup

Preparation time: 20 minutes
Serves 2/Serving size: 1/2 recipe

1	cup canned cannellini beans, rinsed and drained
1	clove garlic, crushed
1	cup sliced celery
2	cups canned Italian plum tomatoes, drained
1 1/2	cups fat-free reduced-sodium chicken broth
1/4	cup uncooked small pasta
1/4	lb lean ham, torn into bite-sized pieces (about 3/4 cup)
	Several drops hot pepper sauce
4–5	sprigs fresh basil, coarsely chopped
2	tsp olive oil
	Salt and freshly ground black pepper to taste
2	Tbsp grated Parmesan cheese

1. Place beans, garlic, celery, and tomatoes in a large pot and add chicken broth. Bring to a boil and cover. Lower heat to medium and simmer for 5 minutes.

2. Add pasta and return to a boil. Boil, uncovered, for 9 minutes or until pasta is cooked, stirring occasionally.

3. Remove from heat and add ham, hot pepper sauce, basil, and olive oil. Stir well.

4. Add salt and pepper.

5. Serve in large soup bowls and sprinkle Parmesan cheese on top.

Nutrition Facts:
Honeydew Melon

Exchanges/Choices
1 Fruit

Calories	60
Calories from Fat	0
Total Fat	0 g
Saturated Fat	0 g
Cholesterol	0 mg
Sodium	30 mg
Carbohydrate	15 g
Dietary Fiber	1 g
Sugars	14 g
Protein	1 g

Honeydew Melon Cubes

1. Serve one cup melon per person.

Dinner

Poultry

Beef

Veal

Pork

Seafood

Chinese Chicken with Cashew Nuts

Brown Rice with Broccoli and Litchi Cup

Stir-fried crisp chicken with cashew nuts is a popular Chinese dish. Chinese recipes have more ingredients than other recipes but take only a few minutes to cook. It's worth a little extra effort for true Chinese flavor.

Toasted sesame oil is available in most supermarkets. Toasting the sesame seeds gives the oil a deep, nutty, sesame flavor. Rice vinegar is a mild condiment made from fermented rice.

Brown rice takes about 45 minutes to cook, but there are several brands of quick-cooking brown rice available. Any quick-cooking rice will work for this dinner.

I call for a small amount of dry sherry in the chicken recipe. You can buy small bottles or splits of sherry at most liquor stores.

Helpful Hints

◆ The secret to crisp, not steamed, stir-frying is to let the ingredients sit for about a minute when you add them to the hot wok before you toss them. This allows the wok to regain its heat after the cold ingredients have been added.

◆ You can use white vinegar diluted with a little water instead of rice vinegar in this recipe.

◆ For easy stir-frying, place all of the prepared ingredients on a cutting board or plate in order of use. You won't have to look at the recipe once you start to cook.

◆ Make sure your wok is very hot before you add the ingredients.

SHOPPING LIST

PRODUCE
1 medium red bell pepper
1 bunch scallions
1 small piece fresh ginger
  (or ground ginger)
1 package broccoli florets
1 medium orange

MEAT
1/2 lb boneless skinless chicken breast

GROCERY
1 small bottle dry sherry
1 small package unsalted cashew nuts
1 can litchis

STAPLES
Garlic
Quick-cooking 30-minute brown rice
Rice vinegar
Lite soy sauce
Sesame oil
Cornstarch
Salt
Black peppercorns

Countdown

◆ Prepare Litchi Cup

◆ Place water for rice on to boil

◆ Marinate chicken

◆ Prepare chicken ingredients

◆ Make rice

◆ Stir-fry chicken

Nutrition Facts:
Chinese Chicken with Cashew Nuts

Exchanges/Choices
1 1/2 Carbohydrate
4 Lean Meat
3 Fat

Calories	372
Calories from Fat	143
Total Fat	16 g
Saturated Fat	4 g
Cholesterol	68 mg
Sodium	1,281 mg
Carbohydrate	21 g
Dietary Fiber	2 g
Sugars	11 g
Protein	30 g

Chinese Chicken with Cashew Nuts

Preparation time: 10 minutes
Serves 2/Serving size: 1/2 recipe

1/4 cup lite soy sauce
1/4 cup rice vinegar
1/4 cup dry sherry
2 Tbsp chopped fresh ginger (or 2 tsp ground ginger)
3 medium cloves garlic, crushed
1/2 lb boneless skinless chicken breast, cut into 1/2-inch pieces
2 tsp sesame oil
1 medium red bell pepper, sliced (1 cup)
1 tsp cornstarch
Salt and freshly ground black pepper to taste
1/4 cup unsalted cashew nuts
2 scallions, sliced

1. Mix soy sauce, vinegar, sherry, ginger, and garlic together in a small bowl. Add chicken and marinate while you prepare the other ingredients.

2. Heat a wok or skillet over high heat and add oil.

3. Remove chicken from marinade with a slotted spoon, reserving liquid. Add chicken to wok and stir-fry 2 minutes. Remove to a plate.

4. Add red bell pepper and stir-fry 2 minutes.

5. Mix cornstarch with reserved marinade. Add marinade and chicken to the wok and stir-fry 2 minutes with the peppers.

6. Remove from heat. Add salt and pepper. Sprinkle cashew nuts and scallions on top and serve over rice.

Nutrition Facts:
Brown Rice with Broccoli

Exchanges/Choices
2 Starch
1 Vegetable
1/2 Fat

Calories	210
Calories from Fat	36
Total Fat	4 g
Saturated Fat	1 g
Cholesterol	0 mg
Sodium	22 mg
Carbohydrate	39 g
Dietary Fiber	4 g
Sugars	1 g
Protein	7 g

Brown Rice with Broccoli

Preparation time: 30 minutes
Serves 2/Serving size: 1/2 recipe

1 1/3 cups water
1/2 cup quick-cooking 30-minute brown rice
2 cups broccoli florets
1 tsp sesame oil
Salt and freshly ground black pepper to taste

1. Bring water to a boil, add rice, lower to medium heat, cover, and cook 25 minutes.

2. Add broccoli florets, cover, and continue to cook 5 minutes. The water should be evaporated. If not, remove the cover and cook a few minutes further. If the rice becomes dry before it is cooked, add more water.

3. Add oil, salt, and pepper.

Nutrition Facts:
Litchi Cup

Exchanges/Choices
1 1/2 Fruit

Calories	98
Calories from Fat	0
Total Fat	0 g
Saturated Fat	0 g
Cholesterol	0 mg
Sodium	0 mg
Carbohydrate	25 g
Dietary Fiber	3 g
Sugars	22 g
Protein	0 g

Litchi Cup

1. Combine 1/2 cup canned litchis, drained, with 1/2 medium orange, peeled and cut into segments.

2. Divide into 2 servings.

Southwestern Chicken

with Tortilla Salad and Spiced Berries

Chunky tomato salsa tops sautéed chicken breasts for this 15-minute meal.

Helpful Hints

- Flattening the chicken helps it to cook faster. If you skip this step, cook the chicken for 8 instead of 5 minutes after it is browned. A meat thermometer should read 160°F.

- Shredded iceberg lettuce and shredded Monterey Jack or Mexican-style cheese are available in most supermarkets and only need to be opened and added to this quick salad. Or use another shredded reduced-fat cheese, such as Swiss or cheddar.

- Choose bottled salsa without added sugar.

- You can use a mixture of berries or one type of berry for dessert.

Countdown

- Make chicken
- Assemble salad
- Make berries

SHOPPING LIST

PRODUCE
1 package washed shredded ready-to-eat lettuce
1 small package blueberries
1 small package strawberries

DAIRY
1 package shredded reduced-fat Monterey Jack cheese

MEAT
3/4 lb boneless skinless chicken breast

GROCERY
1 small jar chunky no-added-sugar tomato salsa
1 can black beans
1 bag tortilla chips

STAPLES
Olive oil cooking spray
Oil and balsamic vinegar salad dressing
Balsamic vinegar
Sugar substitute
Salt
Black peppercorns

Nutrition Facts:
Southwestern Chicken

Exchanges/Choices
5 Lean Meat
1 Vegetable
1/2 Fat

Calories	231
Calories from Fat	40
Total Fat	4 g
Saturated Fat	1 g
Cholesterol	103 mg
Sodium	426 mg
Carbohydrate	6 g
Dietary Fiber	1 g
Sugars	3 g
Protein	39 g

Southwestern Chicken

Preparation time: 10 minutes
Serves 2/Serving size: 1/2 recipe

3/4 lb boneless skinless chicken breast
    Olive oil cooking spray
    Salt and freshly ground black pepper to taste
1 cup bottled chunky no-added-sugar tomato salsa

1. Cut the breasts into two 6-oz portions and flatten the chicken with the bottom of a heavy skillet or the palm of your hand to about 1/2 inch thick.

2. Heat a medium-size nonstick skillet over medium-high heat.

3. Spray skillet with cooking spray and add chicken. Brown 2 minutes on each side. Add salt and pepper to the cooked side. Lower heat to medium low and spoon salsa over each chicken portion. Cover and cook 5 minutes.

4. Serve chicken with salsa on top and Tortilla Salad on the side.

Nutrition Facts:
Tortilla Salad

Exchanges/Choices
2 1/2 Starch
2 Lean Meat
2 Fat

Calories	323
Calories from Fat	136
Total Fat	15 g
Saturated Fat	3 g
Cholesterol	5 mg
Sodium	356 mg
Carbohydrate	36 g
Dietary Fiber	10 g
Sugars	4 g
Protein	12 g

Tortilla Salad
Preparation time: 5 minutes
Serves 2/Serving size: 1/2 recipe

4 cups washed ready-to-eat shredded.iceberg lettuce
1 cup canned black beans, rinsed and drained
2 Tbsp shredded reduced-fat Monterey Jack cheese
2 Tbsp oil and balsamic vinegar salad dressing
1 cup broken tortilla chips

1. Toss iceberg lettuce, black beans, and cheese together in a salad bowl.

2. Add dressing and toss to mix.

3. Sprinkle tortilla chips on top.

Nutrition Facts:
Spiced Berries

Exchanges/Choices
1 Fruit

Calories	70
Calories from Fat	4
Total Fat	0 g
Saturated Fat	0 g
Cholesterol	0 mg
Sodium	4 mg
Carbohydrate	18 g
Dietary Fiber	3 g
Sugars	11 g
Protein	1 g

Spiced Berries
Preparation time: 5 minutes
Serves 2/Serving size: 1/2 recipe

1 1/2 cups mixed berries
(strawberries, blueberries, or raspberries)
1/4 cup balsamic vinegar
Sugar substitute equivalent to 2 tsp

1. Wash berries and divide between two small dessert bowls.

2. Heat balsamic vinegar over high heat for 1 minute or until reduced by one-quarter.

3. Add sugar substitute and stir to dissolve.

4. Pour sauce over berries.

Hungarian Goulash
with Marinated Mushroom Salad

A hearty bowl of soup is welcoming at any time of year. Goulash is a traditional Hungarian dish made with bacon, meat, Hungarian paprika, potatoes, and spices.

The secret to this quick soup is Hungarian paprika. It lends a sweet, peppery flavor to the soup and can be found in the spice section of some supermarkets. Regular paprika will also work well, but be sure your paprika is fresh.

Helpful Hints

◆ If you like a peppery soup, look for hot Hungarian paprika.

◆ You can use any type of lettuce in the mushroom salad.

◆ The soup gains flavor as it sits. Double the recipe and refrigerate or freeze it for another quick dinner.

◆ Use peeled baby carrots to save time.

◆ Slice vegetables in a food processor.

Countdown

◆ Make soup

◆ Marinate mushrooms

◆ Assemble salad

SHOPPING LIST

PRODUCE
1/4 lb portobello mushrooms
1 head Romaine lettuce
1 red onion
1/4 lb russet or Idaho potatoes

DAIRY
1 small carton reduced-fat sour cream

MEAT
3/4 lb smoked turkey breast

GROCERY
Rye bread
1 small bottle caraway seeds
1 bottle Hungarian paprika
1 bottle dried dill
16 oz canned whole tomatoes,
    no added sugar or salt

STAPLES

Celery
Carrots
Garlic
Oil and balsamic vinegar
    salad dressing
Olive oil cooking spray
Salt
Black peppercorns

Nutrition Facts:
Hungarian Goulash

Exchanges/Choices
2 Starch
6 Vegetable
4 Lean Meat
1/2 Fat

Calories	478
Calories from Fat	51
Total Fat	6 g
Saturated Fat	1 g
Cholesterol	65 mg
Sodium	1,966 mg
Carbohydrate	64 g
Dietary Fiber	12 g
Sugars	28 g
Protein	47 g

Hungarian Goulash

Preparation time: 30 minutes
Serves 2/Serving size: 1/2 recipe

	Olive oil cooking spray
2	cups sliced red onion
3	cloves garlic, crushed
1	cup sliced celery
1	cup sliced carrots
1	Tbsp Hungarian paprika
2	tsp caraway seeds
2	cups canned whole tomatoes, no added sugar or salt
1	cup water
1/4	lb russet or Idaho potatoes, cut into 1-inch pieces (about 1 cup)
3/4	lb smoked turkey breast, cut into 2-inch strips (about 2 1/2 cups)
	Salt and freshly ground black pepper to taste
2	medium slices rye bread
2	Tbsp reduced-fat sour cream

1. Spray a large saucepan with cooking spray and place over medium-high heat. Add onion, garlic, celery, and carrots and sauté 5 minutes.

2. Add paprika, caraway seeds, tomatoes, water, and potatoes. Raise heat to high and bring to a boil, breaking up the tomatoes with a spoon. Cover and cook 10 minutes on high heat.

3. Add smoked turkey breast and continue to cook, covered, 5 minutes. Add salt and pepper.

4. Toast bread and serve on the side.

5. Serve soup in large bowls. Top with 1 tablespoon sour cream each.

Marinated Mushroom Salad

Preparation time: 5 minutes
Serves 2/Serving size: 1/2 recipe

Nutrition Facts:
Marinated
Mushroom Salad

Exchanges/Choices
1 Vegetable
1 1/2 Fat

Calories	98
Calories from Fat	75
Total Fat	8 g
Saturated Fat	1 g
Cholesterol	0 mg
Sodium	80 mg
Carbohydrate	4 g
Dietary Fiber	1 g
Sugars	2 g
Protein	2 g

2 cups sliced portobello mushrooms
2 Tbsp oil and balsamic vinegar salad dressing
Several Romaine lettuce leaves
1 tsp dried dill

1. Toss mushrooms in dressing.

2. Wash lettuce leaves and place on serving plate. Spoon mushrooms on top.

3. Sprinkle with dill.

Chicken with Green Peppers and Tomatoes

and Linguine

When I first made this classic dish, Pollo alla Cacciatore, *I asked an Italian friend how to make it. "Don't use red wine; it spoils the dish. Use white wine only," was her emphatic answer. This recipe is a quick 30-minute version of a dish that usually cooks for hours.*

The recipe calls for chicken breasts on the bone. Many markets sell them with the wings and skin removed. This will save you a few extra minutes in your kitchen.

Helpful Hints

◆ You can use any shape whole-wheat pasta.

◆ Use peeled baby carrots to save time.

◆ Slice vegetables in a food processor. Slice mushrooms and remove. Then slice carrots, celery, green pepper, and onion together. This way you will not have to wash the bowl in between.

Countdown

◆ Place water for pasta on to boil

◆ Make chicken

◆ Cook pasta

SHOPPING LIST

PRODUCE
1 medium green pepper
2–3 medium portobello mushrooms

MEAT
2 8-oz chicken breasts with bones

GROCERY
1 jar or can no-added-salt tomato
    or marinara sauce
1/4 lb fresh or dried linguine
1 small bottle extra dry vermouth

STAPLES

Carrots
Parmesan cheese
Onion
Garlic
Olive oil
Salt
Black peppercorns

Nutrition Facts:
Chicken with Green
Peppers and Tomatoes

Exchanges/Choices
5 Vegetable
5 Lean Meat
1 1/2 Fat

Calories	399
Calories from Fat	79
Total Fat	9 g
Saturated Fat	3 g
Cholesterol	117 mg
Sodium	230 mg
Carbohydrate	27 g
Dietary Fiber	5 g
Sugars	21 g
Protein	46 g

Chicken with Green Peppers and Tomatoes
(*Pollo alla Cacciatore*)

Preparation time: 20 minutes
Serves 2/Serving size: 1/2 recipe

- 2 8-oz chicken breasts on the bone, skin, wings, and fat removed
- 1 tsp olive oil
  Salt and freshly ground black pepper to taste
- 1/2 cup extra dry vermouth
- 1/2 small onion, sliced (1/2 cup)
- 1 medium carrot, thinly sliced (1/2 cup)
- 2 medium cloves garlic, crushed
- 1/2 green pepper, sliced (1/2 cup)
- 1 cup sliced portobello mushrooms
- 2 cups no-added-salt tomato or marinara sauce
- 2 Tbsp grated Parmesan cheese

1. Heat oil in a medium-size nonstick skillet over medium-high heat. Brown chicken 2 1/2 minutes per side. Add salt and pepper to cooked side.

2. Remove chicken and pour vermouth into skillet, scraping up all of the brown bits.

3. Add onion and carrot. Cover and simmer for 3 minutes. Lower to medium heat.

4. Add garlic, green pepper, mushrooms, and tomato sauce. Return chicken to skillet and gently simmer, covered, for 5 minutes, or until chicken is cooked through. A meat thermometer should read 180°F.

5. Add salt and pepper.

6. Sprinkle Parmesan cheese on top and serve over linguine.

Nutrition Facts:
Linguine

Exchanges/Choices
3 Starch

Calories	230
Calories from Fat	35
Total Fat	4 g
Saturated Fat	0 g
Cholesterol	0 mg
Sodium	5 mg
Carbohydrate	42 g
Dietary Fiber	3 g
Sugars	2 g
Protein	7 g

Linguine
Preparation time: 10 minutes
Serves 2/Serving size: 1/2 recipe

1/4 lb whole-wheat linguine
  1 tsp olive oil
    Salt and freshly ground black pepper to taste

1. Bring a saucepan with 3–4 quarts water to a boil. Add linguine and boil 9 minutes or according to package instructions.

2. Remove 1/4 cup water from the saucepan and drain linguine. Return linguine to empty pan. Mix olive oil with reserved water and pour over linguine. Toss well.

3. Add salt and pepper.

4. Spoon linguine onto individual plates and serve chicken and sauce over the top.

Mediterranean Meat Loaf

with Garlic-Whipped Potatoes and Mocha Slush

Meat loaf in 20 minutes! Here is a modern variation of one of America's favorite comfort foods. Be sure to look for ground turkey breast in the meat section of the supermarket. Unless it is labeled this way, ground turkey may contain fat and skin.

Helpful Hints

♦ Chop all the ingredients for the meat loaf in a food processor.

♦ The coffee slush tastes best when made at the last minute. Since it takes only minutes to make, prepare it after the main course is finished.

Countdown

♦ Preheat oven to 450°F

♦ Make meat loaf

♦ Make potatoes

♦ Make meat loaf topping

♦ Make coffee slush just before serving

SHOPPING LIST

PRODUCE
1/2 lb yellow potatoes
1 red onion

MEAT
3/4 lb ground turkey breast

GROCERY
1 small can pitted black olives
    (Kalamata if possible)
1 jar crushed red pepper flakes
1 can crushed tomatoes
16 oz fat-free chocolate soda

STAPLES
Carrots
Garlic (16 cloves needed)
Plain bread crumbs
Instant decaffeinated coffee
Eggs
Sugar substitute
Salt
Black peppercorns

Nutrition Facts:
Mediterranean Meat Loaf

Exchanges/Choices
1/2 Starch
5 Vegetable
5 Lean Meat
1/2 Fat

Calories	378
Calories from Fat	37
Total Fat	4 g
Saturated Fat	0 g
Cholesterol	105 mg
Sodium	743 mg
Carbohydrate	34 g
Dietary Fiber	7 g
Sugars	16 g
Protein	49 g

Mediterranean Meat Loaf

Preparation time: 25 minutes
Serves 2/Serving size: 1/2 recipe

1	cup coarsely chopped carrots
1	cup coarsely chopped red onion
1/4	cup plain bread crumbs
3/4	lb ground turkey breast
1	egg white
	Salt and freshly ground black pepper to taste
8	pitted black olives (kalamata if possible), sliced
1/8	tsp crushed red pepper flakes
1	cup canned crushed tomatoes

1. Preheat oven to 450°F.

2. Microwave carrots and onion on high for 3 minutes. They should be slightly shriveled. Mix vegetables with bread crumbs, ground turkey, and egg white. Add salt and pepper. Place a small marble-size piece of the mixture on a plate and microwave 20 seconds. Taste and add more seasoning, if needed.

3. Line a baking sheet with foil. Shape turkey mixture into two 6 × 3-inch loaves. Bake 15 minutes.

4. Meanwhile, mix olives, pepper flakes, and tomatoes together and microwave on high for 2 minutes or until warmed through.

5. Remove meat loaf from oven and serve with tomato mixture on top.

Nutrition Facts:
Garlic-Whipped Potatoes

Exchanges/Choices
2 Starch

Calories	126
Calories from Fat	1
Total Fat	0 g
Saturated Fat	0 g
Cholesterol	0 mg
Sodium	12 mg
Carbohydrate	30 g
Dietary Fiber	3 g
Sugars	7 g
Protein	4 g

Garlic-Whipped Potatoes

Preparation time: 20 minutes
Serves 2/Serving size: 1/2 recipe

- 1/2 lb yellow potatoes
- 16 medium cloves garlic, peeled
- 5 Tbsp water (cooking water from potatoes)
  Salt and freshly ground black pepper to taste

1. Wash potatoes, do not peel, and cut into 1-inch pieces. Place in a medium-size saucepan and add cold water to cover. Cover with a lid and bring to a boil; cook 10 minutes.

2. Add garlic cloves and continue to boil, covered, 5 minutes. Remove 5 Tbsp cooking water and drain potatoes and garlic.

3. Pass potatoes and garlic through a potato ricer or food mill or mash by hand. Whisk in reserved water. If using a food processor, add water and process only until just blended, about 5 seconds.

4. Add salt and pepper and serve with meat loaf.

Nutrition Facts:
Mocha Slush

Exchanges/Choices
1 Free Food

Calories	6
Calories from Fat	0
Total Fat	0 g
Saturated Fat	0 g
Cholesterol	0 mg
Sodium	15 mg
Carbohydrate	1 g
Dietary Fiber	0 g
Sugars	1 g
Protein	0 g

Mocha Slush

Preparation time: 5 minutes
Serves 2/Serving size: 1/2 recipe

- 2 cups fat-free chocolate soda
- 2 tsp decaffeinated instant coffee granules
  Sugar substitute equivalent to 2 tsp
- 30 small ice cubes

1. Blend ingredients until frothy.

Ginger-Minted Chicken

with Lemon and Carrot Barley and Honey Pecan Peaches

If you're in the mood for something different, try this blend of Middle Eastern flavors. Boneless, skinless chicken is marinated in yogurt, spices, mint, and fresh ginger and then broiled. Quick-cooking barley completes the meal. It's flavored with lemon and tossed with shredded carrots, which add a crunchy texture to the dish.

Helpful Hints

◆ Quick-cooking barley is available in the grocery section of the supermarket.

◆ Shredded carrots are available in the produce sections of most supermarkets.

Countdown

◆ Marinate chicken

◆ Preheat broiler

◆ Place water for barley on to boil

◆ Assemble peaches

◆ Cook barley

◆ Broil chicken

◆ Broil peaches

SHOPPING LIST

PRODUCE
1 package shredded carrots
1 bunch fresh mint
1 bunch fresh thyme or
    1 bottle dried thyme
1-inch piece fresh ginger or
    1 bottle ground ginger
1 medium tomato
2 small ripe peaches

DAIRY
1 6-oz carton fat-free plain yogurt

MEAT
2 5-oz boneless skinless chicken
    breast halves

GROCERY
1 package quick-cooking barley
    (in soup section of market)
1 bottle ground coriander
1 small package pecan pieces
1 bottle honey

STAPLES
Garlic   Canola oil
Lemon   Salt
Black peppercorns

108 ◆   Mix 'n' Match Meals in Minutes

Nutrition Facts:
Ginger-Minted Chicken

Exchanges/Choices
1 Fat-Free Milk
1 Vegetable
4 Lean Meat

Calories	270
Calories from Fat	35
Total Fat	4 g
Saturated Fat	1 g
Cholesterol	88 mg
Sodium	195 mg
Carbohydrate	17 g
Dietary Fiber	2 g
Sugars	13 g
Protein	40 g

Ginger-Minted Chicken

Preparation time: 35 minutes
Serves 2/Serving size: 1/2 recipe

1/2 cup coarsely chopped fresh mint
1 1-inch piece fresh ginger, peeled and chopped
(about 1 Tbsp, or use 1 tsp ground ginger)
3 medium cloves garlic, crushed
1 cup fat-free plain yogurt
2 tsp ground coriander
2 5-oz boneless, skinless chicken breast halves
1 medium tomato, sliced

1. Mix mint, ginger, and garlic together in a food processor or small bowl. Add yogurt and coriander.

2. Place chicken in a bowl and pour mixture on top. Marinate 15 minutes, turning once during this time.

3. Preheat broiler.

4. Line a baking sheet with foil and place chicken and marinade on sheet.

5. Broil chicken about 5 inches from the heat source for 5 minutes per side.

6. Serve on bed of Lemon and Carrot Barley with sliced tomatoes along the side.

Lemon and Carrot Barley

Preparation time: 15 minutes
Serves 2/Serving size: 1/2 recipe

Nutrition Facts:
Lemon and Carrot Barley

Exchanges/Choices
2 Starch
1 Vegetable
1 Fat

Calories	215
Calories from Fat	68
Total Fat	**8 g**
Saturated Fat	0 g
Cholesterol	**0 mg**
Sodium	**22 mg**
Carbohydrate	**35 g**
Dietary Fiber	6 g
Sugars	4 g
Protein	**5 g**

    1 1/2 cups water
    1/2 cup quick-cooking barley
      1 cup shredded carrots
      1 Tbsp canola oil
      1 Tbsp chopped fresh thyme (or 1 tsp dried)
      2 Tbsp lemon juice
         Salt and freshly ground black pepper to taste

1. Bring water to a boil and stir in barley. When water returns to a boil, reduce to medium-low heat, partially cover, and simmer 5 minutes. Add carrots, partially cover, and simmer 5 more minutes. If liquid remains, remove cover and boil until it evaporates.

2. Stir oil, thyme, and lemon juice into barley. Add salt and pepper.

Honey Pecan Peaches

Preparation time: 10 minutes
Serves 2/Serving size: 1/2 recipe

Nutrition Facts:
Honey Pecan Peaches

Exchanges/Choices
1 Carbohydrate
1 Fat

Calories	109
Calories from Fat	51
Total Fat	**6 g**
Saturated Fat	0 g
Cholesterol	**0 mg**
Sodium	**0 mg**
Carbohydrate	**16 g**
Dietary Fiber	2 g
Sugars	13 g
Protein	**1 g**

      2 small peaches, pitted and sliced
      2 Tbsp pecan pieces
      2 tsp honey

1. Preheat broiler.

2. Place peaches in a small shallow baking dish.

3. Drizzle honey over peaches and sprinkle pecans on top. Place under broiler 5 inches from the heat source for 5 minutes.

Turkey Chili

with Tossed Salad and Sweet Tequila Sunrise

This is an intriguing, one-pot turkey chili made the Mexican way—with cinnamon. The turkey marinates for a few minutes in cinnamon with a little vinegar. I first noticed the use of cinnamon in Mexican cooking when I saw a friend add some to the meat she was preparing for her chili. Cinnamon is an East Indian spice that found its way to Mexico through Spain. This is a great way to use leftover turkey or chicken.

Helpful Hints

◆ You can use roasted chicken or turkey.

◆ If you're buying roasted turkey at the deli counter, ask for it to be cut in one 1/2-inch slice weighing about 6 oz.

◆ If you do not have tequila on hand, use any type of liqueur over the orange slices.

Countdown

◆ Make chili

◆ Assemble salad

◆ Make dessert

SHOPPING LIST

PRODUCE
1 bunch cilantro
1 orange
1 bag washed ready-to-eat salad mix

DAIRY
1 carton reduced-fat sour cream
1 small container orange juice

MEAT
6 oz cooked turkey breast

GROCERY
1 can red kidney beans
1 can whole tomatoes,
    no added sugar or salt
1 small bottle tequila
1 package frozen chopped onion

STAPLES
Chili powder
Ground cumin
Ground cinnamon
White vinegar
Canola oil
Garlic
Oil and balsamic vinegar
    salad dressing
Salt
Black peppercorns

Nutrition Facts:
Turkey Chili

Exchanges/Choices
2 Starch
3 Vegetable
4 Lean Meat
1 Fat

Calories	415
Calories from Fat	87
Total Fat	10 g
Saturated Fat	3 g
Cholesterol	89 mg
Sodium	306 mg
Carbohydrate	45 g
Dietary Fiber	11 g
Sugars	16 g
Protein	41 g

Turkey Chili

Preparation time: 25 minutes
Serves 2/Serving size: 1/2 recipe

6 oz cooked turkey breast
2 tsp white vinegar
1 tsp ground cinnamon
1 tsp canola oil
1 cup frozen chopped onion
2 medium cloves garlic, crushed
1 cup canned red kidney beans, rinsed and drained
2 cups canned whole tomatoes, no added sugar or salt
1/2 Tbsp chili powder
1 tsp ground cumin
   Salt and freshly ground black pepper to taste
1/2 cup reduced-fat sour cream
1/2 cup fresh chopped cilantro

1. Cut turkey into bite-sized pieces (about 1/2-inch cubes). Place in a bowl and sprinkle with vinegar and cinnamon. Mix well.

2. Heat oil in a medium-size saucepan over medium-high heat. Add onion and garlic. Sauté about 1–2 minutes. They should not be brown.

3. Add kidney beans, tomatoes, chili powder, and cumin. Break up the tomatoes with a spoon. Simmer gently 15 minutes.

4. Add turkey and simmer 5 more minutes. Add salt and pepper and taste for seasoning. Add more chili powder or cumin as needed.

5. Serve chili with sour cream and cilantro on the side.

Nutrition Facts:
Tossed Salad

Exchanges/Choices
1/2 Fat

Calories	35
Calories from Fat	20
Total Fat	2.5 g
Saturated Fat	<1 g
Cholesterol	0 mg
Sodium	150 mg
Carbohydrate	3 g
Dietary Fiber	1 g
Sugars	2 g
Protein	1 g

Tossed Salad
Preparation time: 2 minutes
Serves 2/Serving size: 1/2 recipe

    2 cups washed, ready-to-eat salad
    2 Tbsp reduced-fat oil and vinegar salad dressing

1. Place salad in a bowl and mix in dressing.

Nutrition Facts:
Sweet Tequila Sunrise

Exchanges/Choices
1 Fruit

Calories	63
Calories from Fat	1
Total Fat	0 g
Saturated Fat	0 g
Cholesterol	0 mg
Sodium	0 mg
Carbohydrate	11 g
Dietary Fiber	2 g
Sugars	8 g
Protein	1 g

Sweet Tequila Sunrise
Preparation time: 5 minutes
Serves 2/Serving size: 1/2 recipe

    1 orange
    2 Tbsp tequila
    2 Tbsp orange juice

1. Peel orange and slice.

2. Place slices on two small dessert plates.

3. Mix tequila and orange juice together and spoon over slices.

Middle Eastern Meatballs

with Warm Zucchini Salad

The unusual mixture of sweet spices and meat gives a distinctive flavor to Middle Eastern food. You'll love these broiled meatballs placed in warm pita bread pockets to catch the tasty juices. Spoon some freshly chopped parsley, onion, and a little yogurt into the bread to complete this delicious hot sandwich.

Helpful Hints

◆ You can mix the meatball ingredients in a food processor.

Countdown

◆ Preheat broiler

◆ Make meatballs

◆ Make salad

SHOPPING LIST

PRODUCE
1 bunch fresh parsley
2 small zucchini
1 head Romaine lettuce

DAIRY
1 6-oz carton fat-free plain yogurt

MEAT
1/2 lb lean ground round or sirloin

GROCERY
1 package whole-wheat pita bread
1 can chickpeas

STAPLES

Lemon
Onion
Garlic
Eggs
Raisins
Ground cinnamon
Olive oil
Salt
Black peppercorns

Nutrition Facts:
Middle Eastern Meatballs

Exchanges/Choices
2 Starch
2 Vegetable
3 Lean Meat
1/2 Fruit

Calories	397
Calories from Fat	71
Total Fat	8 g
Saturated Fat	2 g
Cholesterol	76 mg
Sodium	831 mg
Carbohydrate	49 g
Dietary Fiber	5 g
Sugars	15 g
Protein	36 g

Middle Eastern Meatballs

Preparation time: 1 minute
Serves 2/Serving size: 1/2 recipe

1/2	lb lean ground round or sirloin
1	cup plus 2 tsp chopped onion, divided
1	egg white
1	tsp ground cinnamon
1/2	tsp salt
2	Tbsp raisins
2	whole-wheat pita breads
1	cup chopped fresh parsley
2	Tbsp fat-free plain yogurt

1. Preheat broiler and line a baking sheet with foil.

2. Mix ground beef, 1 cup onion, egg white, ground cinnamon, salt, and raisins together. Blend well. To test for seasoning, take a little bit of the mixture and place on a plate or paper towel, microwave on high 20 seconds, and then taste. Add more cinnamon or salt, if necessary.

3. Roll the mixture into meatballs about 2 inches in diameter and place on a baking sheet.

4. Broil about 5 inches from the heat source for 5 minutes and turn the meatballs over. Broil for another 3–4 minutes. If you like your meatballs more well done, then cook 2–3 minutes longer.

5. While meat is cooking, cut pita breads in half. Place bread on a low rack in the same oven as the meat for 5 minutes to warm through.

6. To serve, open the pita bread pockets and divide the meatballs among them. Sprinkle parsley and onion on top and add 1/2 Tbsp yogurt to each. Serve immediately.

Nutrition Facts:
Warm Zucchini Salad

Exchanges/Choices
1 Starch
1 Vegetable
1 1/2 Fat

Calories	156
Calories from Fat	67
Total Fat	7 g
Saturated Fat	1 g
Cholesterol	0 mg
Sodium	69 mg
Carbohydrate	18 g
Dietary Fiber	5 g
Sugars	6 g
Protein	6 g

Warm Zucchini Salad

Preparation time: 10 minutes
Serves 2/Serving size: 1/2 recipe

1	Tbsp lemon juice
2	cloves garlic, crushed
1	Tbsp olive oil
1/2	cup canned chickpeas (garbanzo beans), rinsed and drained
	Salt and freshly ground black pepper to taste
3/4	lb zucchini (about 3 cups)
	Several Romaine lettuce leaves, washed

1. Mix lemon juice and crushed garlic together. Add oil and whisk thoroughly. Add chickpeas, salt, and pepper.

2. Slice zucchini into 1/2-inch rounds. Blanch by bringing a pot half filled with water to a boil and add zucchini. Let water come back to a boil and simmer for 1–2 minutes. Drain and toss in the dressing. Or, microwave on high for 2 minutes and toss with dressing.

3. Serve on a bed of lettuce leaves.

Honey Mustard Beef Kabobs

with Grilled Vegetables and Peach Skewers

You can make these easy-to-fix kabobs in minutes on an outdoor or stove-top grill, or pop them in the broiler. Grilling vegetables gives them a smoky flavor; they can easily be cooked along with the meat.

Helpful Hints

♦ You can use flank, skirt, or another steak suitable for grilling in this recipe.

♦ I call for zucchini and yellow squash, but you can choose a colorful array of whichever vegetables look fresh in the market.

♦ If you broil the kabobs, place them about 2–3 inches from the heat source.

♦ Leave about 1/4 inch between the ingredients on the skewers. This allows the meat and vegetables to cook evenly on all sides.

♦ The peach skewers take only minutes to make. Get them ready to cook, then grill them just before dessert.

♦ Soak wooden skewers in water 10–15 minutes before using them so they don't ignite on the grill.

Countdown

♦ Preheat grill or broiler

♦ Prepare peach skewers

♦ Prepare vegetables and grill

♦ Prepare beef kabobs and grill

♦ Grill peach skewers

SHOPPING LIST

PRODUCE
1/2 lb yellow squash
1/2 lb zucchini
1/2 lb red potatoes
2 medium peaches

MEAT
3/4 lb boneless sirloin steak

GROCERY
1 bottle ground allspice

STAPLES
Olive oil cooking spray
Olive oil
Garlic
Honey
Sugar substitute
Dijon mustard
Worcestershire sauce
Salt
Black peppercorns

Nutrition Facts:
Honey Mustard
Beef Kabobs

Exchanges/Choices
1 Carbohydrate
4 Lean Meat

Calories	288
Calories from Fat	82
Total Fat	9 g
Saturated Fat	3 g
Cholesterol	97 mg
Sodium	1,187 mg
Carbohydrate	14 g
Dietary Fiber	0 g
Sugars	14 g
Protein	38 g

Honey Mustard Beef Kabobs

Preparation time: 10 minutes
Serves 2/Serving size: 1/2 recipe

6 Tbsp Dijon mustard
1 Tbsp honey
1 tsp Worcestershire sauce
    Salt and freshly ground black pepper to taste
3/4 lb boneless sirloin steak, cut into 1-inch cubes

1. Preheat grill or broiler.

2. Combine mustard, honey, and Worcestershire sauce together. Divide mixture, pouring half into two small bowls or ramekins to be used as a dipping sauce.

3. Toss beef cubes in remaining sauce, making sure all sides are coated.

4. Thread beef cubes onto skewers and grill or broil 3 minutes. Turn and grill another 3 minutes.

5. Serve with dipping sauce and vegetables.

Nutrition Facts:
Grilled Vegetables

Exchanges/Choices
1 1/2 Starch
1 Vegetable
1 Fat

Calories	171
Calories from Fat	41
Total Fat	5 g
Saturated Fat	1 g
Cholesterol	0 mg
Sodium	10 mg
Carbohydrate	30 g
Dietary Fiber	5 g
Sugars	6 g
Protein	5 g

Grilled Vegetables

Preparation time: 15 minutes
Serves 2/Serving size: 1/2 recipe

> Olive oil cooking spray
> 1/2 lb yellow squash (about 2 cups sliced)
> 1/2 lb zucchini (about 2 cups sliced)
> 1/2 lb red potatoes (about 2 cups sliced)
> 2 tsp olive oil
> 1 medium clove garlic, crushed
> 1/2 Tbsp water
> Salt and freshly ground black pepper to taste

1. Preheat grill or broiler and spray with cooking spray.

2. Wash squash, zucchini, and potatoes. Cut ends off squash and zucchini and cut in half lengthwise. Slice into 1/4-inch strips, yielding four to five long strips. Cut potato lengthwise into 1/4-inch slices.

3. Mix olive oil with garlic, water, salt, and pepper together in a medium bowl. Add vegetables and toss to make sure all sides are coated.

4. Place vegetables in one layer on grill or broiler pan. Grill or broil 3 minutes, turn vegetables over, and grill or broil 3 minutes more. Remove to a bowl. Cover with foil to keep warm.

Nutrition Facts:
Peach Skewers

Exchanges/Choices
1 Fruit

Calories	48
Calories from Fat	1
Total Fat	0 g
Saturated Fat	0 g
Cholesterol	0 mg
Sodium	0 mg
Carbohydrate	12 g
Dietary Fiber	2 g
Sugars	10 g
Protein	1 g

Peach Skewers

Preparation time: 10 minutes
Serves 2/Serving size: 1/2 recipe

> 2 medium peaches
> 1/4 tsp ground allspice
> Sugar substitute equivalent to 2 tsp

1. Preheat grill or broiler.

2. Slice peaches in half and remove pit. Cut each half into three large slices.

3. Mix allspice and sugar substitute together and toss peach slices in mixture, making sure all of the slices are coated.

4. Place slices on skewers and grill or broil 3 minutes, turn fruit over, and grill or broil 3 minutes more.

5. Serve warm.

Chinese Pepper Steak

with Quick Stir-Fried Rice and Pineapple Chunks

You'll be stir-frying thin slices of beef in a savory mixture of green peppers, fresh ginger, and garlic to make this tasty dish. Chinese food takes only minutes to cook; it's the chopping and cutting that take some time. To speed things up, look for pre-sliced beef and stir-fry vegetables in the supermarket. Or slice vegetables in a food processor.

Use the same wok to make the rice—the pan juices from the meat will flavor it. Fried rice is great made with leftover rice.

Helpful Hints

♦ You can use skirt or flank steak instead of sirloin.

♦ You'll need chopped onion for both recipes, so prepare it all at once and divide accordingly.

♦ Your wok or skillet should be very hot when you add the vegetables and meat.

Countdown

♦ Place water for rice on to boil

♦ Prepare beef ingredients

♦ Boil rice

♦ Stir-fry beef

♦ Stir-fry rice

SHOPPING LIST
PRODUCE
2 medium green bell peppers
1 small piece fresh ginger
1 package fresh pineapple chunks

MEAT
1/2 lb sirloin steak

STAPLES
Long-grain white rice
Onion
Garlic
Sesame oil
Lite soy sauce
Salt
Black peppercorns

Nutrition Facts:
Chinese Pepper Steak

Exchanges/Choices
3 Vegetable
3 Lean Meat

Calories	242
Calories from Fat	69
Total Fat	8 g
Saturated Fat	2 g
Cholesterol	64 mg
Sodium	661 mg
Carbohydrate	19 g
Dietary Fiber	4 g
Sugars	11 g
Protein	25 g

Chinese Pepper Steak

Preparation time: 10 minutes
Serves 2/Serving size: 1/2 recipe

- 1 tsp sesame oil
- 1/2 medium onion, sliced (1 cup)
- 2 medium green bell peppers, sliced (about 3 cups)
- 1 Tbsp chopped fresh ginger or 1 tsp ground ginger
- 3 medium cloves garlic, crushed
- 1/2 lb sirloin steak, cut into two 5 1/2-inch strips
- 2 Tbsp lite soy sauce

1. Heat sesame oil in wok over high heat. When wok is smoking, add onion, green pepper, ginger, and garlic. Stir-fry 3 minutes.

2. Add meat and stir-fry 1 minute.

3. Add soy sauce and stir-fry 3 minutes. Remove to a plate. Do not wash wok; use it to stir-fry cooked rice.

Nutrition Facts:
Quick Stir-Fried Rice

Exchanges/Choices
2 1/2 Starch
1/2 Fat

Calories	201
Calories from Fat	44
Total Fat	5 g
Saturated Fat	1 g
Cholesterol	0 mg
Sodium	2 mg
Carbohydrate	35 g
Dietary Fiber	1 g
Sugars	1 g
Protein	3 g

Quick Stir-Fried Rice

Preparation time: 15 minutes
Serves 2/Serving size: 1/2 recipe

1/2 cup long-grain white rice
2 tsp sesame oil
1/4 cup sliced onion
    Salt and freshly ground black pepper to taste

1. Bring a large pot with 2–3 quarts of water to a boil. Add rice and boil, uncovered, about 10 minutes. Test a grain. Rice should be cooked through but not soft. Drain into a colander in the sink.

2. Add oil to wok and heat to smoking. Add onion and stir-fry 1 minute. Add rice and stir-fry 2–3 minutes. Add salt and pepper.

Nutrition Facts:
Pineapple Chunks

Exchanges/Choices
1/2 Fruit

Calories	39
Calories from Fat	3
Total Fat	0.5 g
Saturated Fat	0 g
Cholesterol	0 mg
Sodium	1 mg
Carbohydrate	9 g
Dietary Fiber	1 g
Sugars	7 g
Protein	0 g

Pineapple Chunks

1. Serve 1/2 cup per person.

Korean Grilled Beef

with Green Rice and Almond-Stuffed Pears

Steak plays an important role in Korean cooking, unlike other Asian cuisines. Invading Mongols brought beef to Korea in the Middle Ages. Rice cooked with spinach and bean sprouts is another Korean staple. I have adapted these recipes to showcase the intriguing flavors of Korean cooking while reducing preparation time.

Helpful Hints

◆ You can use flank, strip, or sirloin instead of skirt steak.

◆ This beef works well on an outdoor or stove-top grill, or you can broil it.

◆ Most washed, ready-to-eat spinach is sold in 10-oz bags. Use half a bag for this recipe.

Countdown

◆ Marinate beef

◆ Make pears

◆ Make rice

◆ Preheat grill or broiler

◆ Grill beef

SHOPPING LIST

PRODUCE
1 bunch scallions
1 5-oz package washed
    ready-to-eat spinach
1 package fresh bean sprouts
2 small ripe pears
1 small bunch fresh mint (optional)

MEAT
3/4 lb skirt steak

GROCERY
1 bottle almond extract
1 small package slivered almonds

STAPLES

Garlic
Dijon mustard
White vinegar
Lite soy sauce
Sesame oil
Quick-cooking brown rice
Salt
Black peppercorns

Nutrition Facts:
Korean Grilled Beef

Exchanges/Choices
4 Lean Meat

Calories	220
Calories from Fat	67
Total Fat	7 g
Saturated Fat	3 g
Cholesterol	97 mg
Sodium	557 mg
Carbohydrate	2 g
Dietary Fiber	0 g
Sugars	2 g
Protein	34 g

Korean Grilled Beef

Preparation time: 25 minutes
Serves 2/Serving size: 1/2 recipe

> 3/4 lb skirt steak
> 2 Tbsp lite soy sauce
> 2 Tbsp white vinegar
> 2 cloves garlic, crushed
> 2 tsp Dijon mustard
> Salt and freshly ground black pepper to taste

1. Score meat deeply crosswise at 1/2-inch intervals. This allows the meat to absorb more of the marinade and cook more evenly.

2. Mix soy sauce, vinegar, garlic, and mustard together. Add meat and turn in the marinade to make sure all sides are coated with the sauce. Marinate for 10 minutes.

3. Preheat grill or broiler. Remove meat and discard marinade. Place on grill or broiler about 3–4 inches from the heat source. Grill 5–7 minutes. A meat thermometer should read 145°F. Remove to a carving board and add salt and pepper to the cooked steak.

4. Slice steak across the grain, making sure to capture the juices.

5. Serve over Green Rice, and pour the juices on top.

Green Rice

Preparation time: 35 minutes
Serves 2/Serving size: 1/2 recipe

- 5 oz washed ready-to-eat fresh spinach
- 1/2 cup quick-cooking brown rice
- 1 cup fresh bean sprouts
- 1 cup water
- 2 tsp sesame oil
- 2 scallions, sliced
- Salt and freshly ground black pepper to taste

1. Place spinach, rice, bean sprouts, and water in a large saucepan. Bring the water to a boil and cover with a lid. Lower heat to medium and simmer 30 minutes or according to package instructions. The water should be absorbed and the rice cooked through. If the rice is cooked and there is still liquid in the pan, remove lid and boil to evaporate liquid.

2. Stir in sesame oil and scallions. Add salt and pepper.

3. Place on dinner plate. Serve sliced steak on top.

Nutrition Facts:
Green Rice

Exchanges/Choices
1 1/2 Starch
1 Vegetable
1 Fat

Calories	171
Calories from Fat	51
Total Fat	6 g
Saturated Fat	1 g
Cholesterol	0 mg
Sodium	72 mg
Carbohydrate	27 g
Dietary Fiber	4 g
Sugars	2 g
Protein	6 g

Almond-Stuffed Pears

Preparation time: 5 minutes
Serves 2/Serving size: 1/2 recipe

- 2 small ripe pears
- 2 Tbsp slivered almonds
- 2 tsp almond extract
- Garnish
- Mint leaves (optional)

1. Slice pears in half and remove core. Cut a thin slice from the rounded side of the pear so that it will sit flat.

2. Toast slivered almonds in a toaster oven until slightly golden, about 30 seconds.

3. Place pear halves on two small dessert plates and sprinkle almond extract in the cored center of each half.

4. Spoon slivered almonds in the cored center and place sprig of mint on the side.

Nutrition Facts:
Almond-Stuffed Pears

Exchanges/Choices
1 1/2 Fruit
1 Fat

Calories	141
Calories from Fat	42
Total Fat	5 g
Saturated Fat	0 g
Cholesterol	0 mg
Sodium	1 mg
Carbohydrate	23 g
Dietary Fiber	4 g
Sugars	18 g
Protein	2 g

Picadillo

with Tomato and Onion Salad and Cheddar Cheese and Apples

Picadillo, or ground meat in a flavor-packed tomato sauce, is a popular Cuban dish served in many Latin restaurants. There are many Picadillo variations, but olives and capers are usually part of the recipe. It was served at Sloppy Joe's Bar in Key West over rolls and became known there as Sloppy Joes. On a roll or not, it's a quick and delicious dish that can be made a day ahead or frozen for later.

Helpful Hints

◆ Look for lean ground round or sirloin.

◆ To quickly chop fresh herbs, wash, dry, and snip the leaves with scissors right off the stem.

◆ You'll need chopped onion for both recipes, so prepare it all at once and divide accordingly.

◆ If you are pressed for time, use frozen chopped onion and green pepper.

Countdown

◆ Make picadillo

◆ Make salad

◆ Assemble dessert

SHOPPING LIST

PRODUCE
1 red onion
1 medium green bell pepper
2 medium tomatoes

DAIRY
1 small package reduced-fat
    sharp cheddar cheese

MEAT
1/2 lb lean ground round

GROCERY
1 can tomato sauce (12 oz needed)
1 small jar capers

STAPLES
Lemon
Apples
Olive oil
Oil and balsamic vinegar
    salad dressing
Garlic
Worcestershire sauce
White vinegar
Salt
Black peppercorns

Nutrition Facts:
Picadillo

Exchanges/Choices
1 Starch
5 Vegetable
3 Lean Meat

Calories	359
Calories from Fat	63
Total Fat	7 g
Saturated Fat	2 g
Cholesterol	58 mg
Sodium	581 mg
Carbohydrate	45 g
Dietary Fiber	6 g
Sugars	23 g
Protein	28 g

Picadillo

Preparation time: 20 minutes
Serves 2/Serving size: 1/2 recipe

1	tsp olive oil
1	cup diced red onion
2	cloves garlic, crushed
1	cup diced green bell pepper
1/2	lb lean ground round
1 1/2	cups canned tomato sauce
1	Tbsp drained capers
2	Tbsp Worcestershire sauce
2	Tbsp white vinegar
	Salt and freshly ground pepper to taste
2	small whole-wheat rolls

1. Heat oil in a nonstick skillet over medium-high heat. Add onion, garlic, and green pepper. Sauté for 5 minutes.

2. Add beef and brown, breaking it up into small pieces as it browns. Drain fat.

3. Add tomato sauce and mix well. Add capers, Worcestershire sauce, and white vinegar. Lower heat to medium and cook at a simmer, stirring occasionally, until meat is cooked through, about 10 minutes.

4. Taste for seasoning. Add salt and pepper and more vinegar and Worcestershire sauce, if necessary.

5. Serve on rolls.

Nutrition Facts:
Tomato and Onion Salad

Exchanges/Choices
2 Vegetable
1 1/2 Fat

Calories	114
Calories from Fat	77
Total Fat	9 g
Saturated Fat	1 g
Cholesterol	0 mg
Sodium	89 mg
Carbohydrate	9 g
Dietary Fiber	2 g
Sugars	6 g
Protein	1 g

Tomato and Onion Salad

Preparation time: 5 minutes
Serves 2/Serving size: 1/2 recipe

- 2 medium tomatoes, sliced
- 1/4 cup diced red onion
- 2 Tbsp oil and balsamic vinegar salad dressing
- Salt and freshly ground black pepper

1. Arrange tomatoes on a serving plate.

2. Sprinkle diced onion on top of tomatoes and drizzle dressing over both.

3. Add salt and pepper.

Nutrition Facts:
Cheddar Cheese and Apples

Exchanges/Choices
1 Medium-Fat Meat
1 Fruit

Calories	145
Calories from Fat	58
Total Fat	6 g
Saturated Fat	4 g
Cholesterol	20 mg
Sodium	242 mg
Carbohydrate	17 g
Dietary Fiber	3 g
Sugars	14 g
Protein	7 g

Cheddar Cheese and Apples

Preparation time: 5 minutes
Serves 2/Serving size: 1/2 recipe

- 2 small apples
- 1 Tbsp lemon juice
- 2 oz reduced-fat sharp cheddar cheese

1. Core apples and cut into thin slices.

2. Divide slices between two small dessert plates.

3. Sprinkle with lemon juice.

4. Cut cheese into strips and serve over slices.

Stuffed Veal Rolls

with Parmesan Tomatoes and Beans and Strawberry-Banana Cup

Stuffed veal rolls are a popular dish in Emilia-Romagna, a rich and fertile area of Northern Italy where veal is a specialty.

Helpful Hints

♦ You can use a good-quality cheddar or Swiss cheese instead of Parmesan.

♦ Buy good-quality Parmesan cheese and ask the market to grate it for you or chop it in the food processor. Freeze extra for quick use. You can spoon out the quantity you need and leave the rest frozen.

♦ You can use any type of canned white beans.

♦ Make sure your veal cutlets are about the same size. If not, cut the bigger pieces to match the smaller ones. They will cook more evenly this way.

♦ You can turn the veal rolls easily with kitchen tongs.

Countdown

♦ Prepare fruit

♦ Make beans and cover with a lid to keep warm

♦ Make veal

SHOPPING LIST

PRODUCE
1 bunch arugula
1 bunch basil
2 medium tomatoes
1 small container strawberries
1 medium banana

MEAT
1/2 lb veal cutlets, thinly cut

GROCERY
1 can cannellini beans

STAPLES
Extra-dry vermouth
Parmesan cheese
Fat-free reduced-sodium
    chicken broth
Olive oil
Salt
Black peppercorns

Stuffed Veal Rolls

Preparation time: 15 minutes
Serves 2/Serving size: 1/2 recipe

	Nutrition Facts: Stuffed Veal Rolls

Nutrition Facts:
Stuffed Veal Rolls

Exchanges/Choices
4 Lean Meat
1/2 Fat

Calories	256
Calories from Fat	65
Total Fat	7 g
Saturated Fat	2 g
Cholesterol	134 mg
Sodium	197 mg
Carbohydrate	2 g
Dietary Fiber	1 g
Sugars	0 g
Protein	38 g

3/4 lb thinly cut veal cutlets, fat trimmed
    Salt and freshly ground black pepper to taste
1 bunch arugula (1 cup), washed and patted dry
1 bunch basil (1 cup), washed and patted dry
1 tsp olive oil
1/2 cup extra-dry vermouth
1/2 cup fat-free reduced-sodium chicken broth

1. Spread the veal out on a cutting board or countertop and flatten with a meat mallet or bottom of a heavy skillet to 1/4-inch thick. Salt and pepper the veal pieces.

2. Place a layer of arugula over the veal, making sure the surface is covered. Place a layer of basil leaves over the arugula. Roll up meat and fasten with a wooden toothpick.

3. Heat oil in a nonstick skillet just large enough to hold the veal in one layer. Brown veal rolls on all sides, about 3 minutes. Remove to a dish and cover with foil to keep warm.

4. Add vermouth to the skillet. Let reduce about 2 minutes, scraping up the brown bits as it cooks. Add broth. Let reduce again about 5 minutes. Return veal to the sauce to let it warm through for a minute. If rolls are thick, warm for 3–4 minutes.

5. Remove rolls and slice into 2-inch pieces. Place on plates with the sliced side up so that the colorful interior shows. Spoon sauce over the top.

Nutrition Facts:
Parmesan Tomatoes
and Beans

Exchanges/Choices	
1 Starch	
1 Lean Meat	

Calories	123
Calories from Fat	24
Total Fat	3 g
Saturated Fat	1 g
Cholesterol	5 mg
Sodium	231 mg
Carbohydrate	19 g
Dietary Fiber	5 g
Sugars	5 g
Protein	8 g

Parmesan Tomatoes and Beans

Preparation time: 10 minutes
Serves 2/Serving size: 1/2 recipe

- 1/2 cup fat-free reduced-sodium chicken broth
- 1/2 cup canned cannellini beans, rinsed and drained
- 2 medium tomatoes, diced (about 2 cups)
- 2 Tbsp grated Parmesan cheese
  Salt and freshly ground black pepper to taste

1. Add broth, beans, and tomatoes to a medium-size saucepan. Bring to a simmer. Cook 5 minutes or until beans and tomatoes are warmed through.

2. Add Parmesan cheese, salt, and pepper. Toss well.

Nutrition Facts:
Strawberry-Banana Cup

Exchanges/Choices	
2 Fruit	

Calories	115
Calories from Fat	10
Total Fat	1 g
Saturated Fat	0.2 g
Cholesterol	0 mg
Sodium	3 mg
Carbohydrate	28 g
Dietary Fiber	4 g
Sugars	17 g
Protein	8 g

Strawberry-Banana Cup

1. Serve 1/2 cup sliced fresh strawberries mixed with 1/4 cup sliced bananas per person.

Veal Gorgonzola

with Fresh Linguine and Artichoke Hearts with Frozen Yogurt

Veal with Gorgonzola sauce is a perfect blend of the ingredients from the Lombardy region in northern Italy that stretches to the Alps. Gorgonzola is a blue-veined, mild cheese that takes its name from the town of that name in Lombardy. A domestic Gorgonzola works very well in the recipe and is easily found in the supermarket.

Helpful Hints

◆ Look for crumbled, domestic Gorgonzola in the dairy section of the market.

◆ Any type of blue-veined cheese can be used.

◆ Any type of mushroom can be used.

◆ Marinated artichoke hearts can be found in most supermarkets.

◆ Use a nonstick skillet that just fits the veal in one layer. If it is too big, the sauce will evaporate.

Countdown

◆ Make pasta

◆ Make veal

SHOPPING LIST

DAIRY
1 small package crumbled
    Gorgonzola cheese (1 oz needed)

MEAT
2 4-oz veal cutlets

GROCERY
1 small package fresh or dried
    spinach linguine (1/4 lb needed)
1 6-oz jar/can marinated artichokes
1 small container frozen
    low-fat yogurt

PRODUCE
1 package sliced baby bello mushrooms

STAPLES
Flour
Olive oil
Olive oil spray
Fat-free milk
Salt
Black peppercorns

Nutrition Facts:
Veal Gorgonzola

Exchanges/Choices
1/2 Carbohydrate
4 Lean Meat

Calories	195
Calories from Fat	40
Total Fat	4.5 g
Saturated Fat	2 g
Cholesterol	95 mg
Sodium	140 mg
Carbohydrate	8 g
Dietary Fiber	0 g
Sugars	4 g
Protein	29 g

Veal Gorgonzola

Preparation time: 10 minutes
Serves: 2/Serving size: 1/2 recipe

- 1 Tbsp flour
  Salt and fresh ground black pepper
- 2 4-oz veal cutlets
  Olive oil spray
- 1 cup sliced baby bello mushrooms
- 1/2 cup fat-free milk
- 1 Tbsp crumbled Gorgonzola cheese

1. Place flour on a plate and season with salt and pepper to taste.

2. Dip the veal cutlets in the flour making sure both sides are coated.

3. Heat a small nonstick skillet over medium-high heat and spray with olive oil spray. Add the veal. Brown 2 minutes and turn over. Brown the second side 1 minute. Transfer to a serving dish and sprinkle with salt and pepper to taste.

4. Add mushrooms and sauté 1 minute.

5. Add the milk to the skillet and scrape up the brown bits in the bottom of the pan.

6. Immediately add the Gorgonzola cheese and stir to melt the cheese and make a smooth sauce. Cook to reduce and thicken sauce, about 2–3 minutes. Taste for seasoning. Add pepper if needed. The cheese should provide enough salt.

7. Spoon sauce over cutlets and serve.

Nutrition Facts:
Fresh Linguine with
Artichoke Hearts

Exchanges/Choices
2 Starch
1 Vegetable
1 Fat

Calories	225
Calories from Fat	55
Total Fat	6 g
Saturated Fat	0.7 g
Cholesterol	0 mg
Sodium	260 mg
Carbohydrate	34 g
Dietary Fiber	2 g
Sugars	1 g
Protein	8 g

Fresh Linguine with Artichoke Hearts

Preparation time: 12 minutes
Serves: 2/Serving size: 1/2 recipe

- 1/4 lb fresh spinach linguine
- 1 tsp olive oil
- 3/4 cup drained, marinated artichoke hearts
  (cut into small pieces)
  Salt and freshly ground black pepper

1. Place a large saucepan with 3–4 quarts water on to boil.

2. Add linguine and boil 3 minutes if fresh, 9 minutes if dried.

3. Drain, leaving about 2 Tbsp water on pasta.

4. Add oil, artichoke hearts, and salt and pepper to taste. Toss well.

Nutrition Facts:
Frozen Yogurt

Exchanges/Choices
1 1/2 Carbohydrate

Calories	120
Calories from Fat	27
Total Fat	3 g
Saturated Fat	1.5 g
Cholesterol	10 mg
Sodium	80 mg
Carbohydrate	20 g
Dietary Fiber	0 g
Sugars	14 g
Protein	3 g

Frozen Yogurt

1 cup frozen low-fat yogurt (any flavor)

1. Divide between two dessert bowls, giving 1/2 cup per person.

Mojo Roasted Pork

with Cuban Rice and Beans and Pears with Pineapple Sauce

Caribbean restaurants have become popular in many cities throughout the States. I have created these flavorful, simple, Cuban-style recipes that you can make at home in minutes.

A garlicky mojo glaze coats this pan-roasted pork tenderloin. Mojo is a Cuban condiment and marinade that is used in many Cuban recipes. There are many versions, but it's usually made with Seville or sour oranges, spices, garlic, onion, and oil. You can find it bottled in most supermarkets, sometimes under the name Spanish barbecue sauce. The bottled version is perfect for this quick pork dinner. Look for one that is low in fat. Some have no fat.

If you can't find mojo in your store, use this quick substitute. It's not very authentic, but it works well for this recipe: mix together 1/4 cup orange juice, 1/4 cup lemon or lime juice, and 3 garlic cloves, crushed; add a little salt and pepper and use as the marinade. (The nutrition analysis for the pork was calculated using this recipe without added salt or pepper.)

Helpful Hints

♦ You can use red beans instead of black.

♦ Look for rum in small splits similar to the size served on airplanes. Or, use an orange-flavored liqueur.

♦ To save time, measure the mojo sauce in a glass liquid measuring cup and marinate the pork in the cup.

Countdown

♦ Marinate pork

♦ Set water for rice on to boil

♦ Make rice

♦ Make pork

♦ Make dessert

SHOPPING LIST

PRODUCE
1 ripe medium pear
1 medium green bell pepper
1 small package fresh pineapple cubes
1 small bunch fresh mint (optional)

MEAT
3/4 lb pork tenderloin

GROCERY
1 small bottle mojo sauce
1 bottle low-sugar apricot spread
1 can black beans
1 small bottle or 1 split light rum

STAPLES
Onion
Canola oil
Quick-cooking 30-minute brown rice
Sugar substitute
Salt
Black peppercorns

Nutrition Facts:
Mojo Roasted Pork

Exchanges/Choices
1/2 Carbohydrate
4 Lean Meat

Calories	241
Calories from Fat	56
Total Fat	6 g
Saturated Fat	2 g
Cholesterol	97 mg
Sodium	84 mg
Carbohydrate	10 g
Dietary Fiber	0 g
Sugars	8 g
Protein	36 g

Mojo Roasted Pork

Preparation time: 25 minutes
Serves 2/Serving size: 1/2 recipe

3/4 lb pork tenderloin
1/2 cup mojo sauce
1 Tbsp low-sugar apricot spread

1. Remove fat from pork and butterfly it by cutting the pork in half lengthwise and opening it like a book. Do not cut all the way through. Place pork in the mojo and let marinate for 15 minutes.

2. Heat a nonstick skillet over medium-high heat. Remove pork, reserving marinade. Pat dry with paper towel and sauté in skillet 3 minutes. Turn and sauté 3 minutes. The pork is done when a meat thermometer reads 160°F.

3. Mix reserved marinade and apricot spread together. Remove pork to a plate and add marinade mixture to the skillet. Boil about 1 minute, scraping up the brown bits in the pan as it boils. Divide pork into two portions, place on dinner plates, and spoon sauce over the top.

Nutrition Facts:
Cuban Rice and Beans

Exchanges/Choices
2 Starch
1 Vegetable
2 Fat

Calories	252
Calories from Fat	90
Total Fat	**10 g**
Saturated Fat	1 g
Cholesterol	**0 mg**
Sodium	**91 mg**
Carbohydrate	**35 g**
Dietary Fiber	8 g
Sugars	5 g
Protein	**8 g**

Cuban Rice and Beans

Preparation time: 35 minutes
Serves 2/Serving size: 1/2 recipe

1/3 cup quick-cooking 30-minute brown rice
1/2 cup sliced onion
  1 cup green bell pepper, sliced
3/4 cup canned black beans, rinsed and drained
  4 tsp canola oil
     Salt and freshly ground black pepper to taste

1. Bring a large saucepan with 2–3 quarts of water to a boil. Add rice and boil rapidly 27 minutes.

2. Add onion and pepper and continue to boil 3 minutes or until the rice is cooked through but still firm.

3. Drain rice mixture and place in a bowl. Add black beans and oil and toss well. Add salt and pepper.

Nutrition Facts:
Pears with Pineapple Sauce

Exchanges/Choices
1 Fruit

Calories	77
Calories from Fat	4
Total Fat	**0 g**
Saturated Fat	0 g
Cholesterol	**0 mg**
Sodium	**0 mg**
Carbohydrate	**18 g**
Dietary Fiber	2 g
Sugars	15 g
Protein	**0 g**

Pears with Pineapple Sauce

Preparation time: 5 minutes
Serves 2/Serving size: 1/2 recipe

  1 ripe medium pear
1/2 cup fresh pineapple cubes
     Sugar substitute equivalent to 1 tsp
1/2 Tbsp light rum
     Several mint leaves for garnish (optional)

1. Slice pear in half and remove core. Cut a thin slice from the rounded side of the pear so that it will sit flat. Place on two dessert plates, rounded side down.

2. Purée pineapple, sugar substitute, and rum together in a food processor or blender. Spoon over pears.

3. Place mint leaves on the side for garnish.

Cider Pork

with Autumn Squash and Apricot Fool

When I saw the markets filled with autumn colors and flavors, golden jugs of cider, green and orange squash, and an array of colorful nuts, I was inspired to create this Cider Pork. It's simple to make and I find the apple flavor enhances the pork and rosemary.

Helpful Hints

◆ To save time, wash the squash but do not peel it.

◆ To quickly chop fresh rosemary, wash, dry, and snip the leaves with scissors right off the stem.

◆ You can use frozen uncooked squash or pumpkin cubes. Simply sauté the onions, add the frozen squash, and cook until defrosted.

◆ Sauté the squash and then let it finish cooking in the heat of the pan off the burner. This method allows the squash to develop its delicate texture while you prepare the rest of the meal.

Countdown

◆ Make squash

◆ Make pork

◆ Make dessert

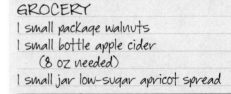

SHOPPING LIST

PRODUCE
1 bunch fresh rosemary or
   1 bottle dried rosemary
1 small acorn squash

DAIRY
1 small carton fat-free artificially
   sweetened apricot-flavored yogurt

MEAT
3/4 lb pork tenderloin

GROCERY
1 small package walnuts
1 small bottle apple cider
   (8 oz needed)
1 small jar low-sugar apricot spread

STAPLES
Onion
Olive oil
Sugar substitute
Salt
Black peppercorns

Nutrition Facts:
Cider Pork

Exchanges/Choices
4 Lean Meat
1 Fruit

Calories	305
Calories from Fat	99
Total Fat	11 g
Saturated Fat	3 g
Cholesterol	97 mg
Sodium	75 mg
Carbohydrate	15 g
Dietary Fiber	1 g
Sugars	13 g
Protein	35 g

Cider Pork

Preparation time: 20 minutes
Serves 2/Serving size: 1/2 recipe

> 3/4 lb pork tenderloin
> 1 Tbsp fresh rosemary (or 2 tsp dried)
> 2 tsp olive oil
> Salt and freshly ground black pepper to taste
> 1 cup apple cider

1. Remove fat from pork. Butterfly pork by cutting in half lengthwise and opening like a book. Do not cut all the way though. Cut in half crosswise to make two pieces.

2. Sprinkle with rosemary.

3. Heat oil over medium-high heat in a nonstick skillet just big enough to snugly fit the pork. Brown pork on both sides, about 5 minutes total. Salt and pepper the cooked sides.

4. Add cider to the skillet and bring to a simmer. Cover pan with a lid and cook on low for 10 minutes.

5. Remove pork to a plate and raise heat to high. Reduce liquid by half, then spoon sauce over pork.

Exchanges/Choices
1 1/2 Starch
1 Vegetable
1 Fat

Calories	182
Calories from Fat	65
Total Fat	7 g
Saturated Fat	1 g
Cholesterol	0 mg
Sodium	9 mg
Carbohydrate	30 g
Dietary Fiber	9 g
Sugars	12 g
Protein	3 g

Autumn Squash

Preparation time: 25 minutes
Serves 2/Serving size: 1/2 recipe

2 tsp olive oil
1 cup fresh or frozen chopped onion
2 cups cubed acorn squash (1/2-inch cubes)
1 Tbsp broken walnuts
Salt and freshly ground black pepper to taste

1. Heat oil in a medium-size saucepan over medium-high heat.

2. Sauté onions and squash for 8 minutes, stirring several times.

3. Add walnuts and sauté 2 more minutes. Add salt and pepper.

4. Cover and remove from heat. Let sit, covered, for at least 10 minutes or until ready to serve.

Nutrition Facts:
Apricot Fool

Exchanges/Choices
1/2 Milk
1 Carbohydrate

Calories	120
Calories from Fat	0
Total Fat	0 g
Saturated Fat	0 g
Cholesterol	2 mg
Sodium	87 mg
Carbohydrate	25 g
Dietary Fiber	0 g
Sugars	19 g
Protein	5 g

Apricot Fool

Preparation time: 5 minutes
Serves 2/Serving size: 1/2 recipe

1/4 cup low-sugar apricot spread
1 cup fat-free artificially sweetened apricot-flavored yogurt
Sugar substitute to the equivalent of 2 tsp

1. Whisk apricot spread in a small bowl.

2. Add yogurt and sugar substitute and whisk until blended. Spoon into small dessert bowls.

Italian Roast Pork

with Herbed Garlic Lentils and Grapefruit with Toasted Pine Nuts

This Italian Roast Pork is a simple recipe that goes well with the Herbed Garlic Lentils. Try lentils for a change from rice and other grains. They take only 20 minutes to cook and don't need presoaking.

Helpful Hints

♦ Garlic is used in both recipes, so crush it all at once and divide accordingly.

♦ A quick way to peel a grapefruit is to cut off each end down to the fruit. Stand the grapefruit on a cut end and slice the skin off the sides from top to bottom. Turn on its side and cut into six slices.

♦ Do not overcook the pork or it will become dry and tough. Contrary to what we were all taught when we were younger, pork can be slightly pink inside. A meat thermometer should read 160°F.

Countdown

♦ Make lentils

♦ Preheat oven

♦ Roast pork

♦ Make dessert

SHOPPING LIST

PRODUCE
1 small bunch fresh sage or
   1 bottle ground sage
2 medium tomatoes
1 grapefruit

MEAT
3/4 lb pork tenderloin

GROCERY
1 small package dried lentils
1 small package pine nuts

STAPLES

Fat-free reduced-sodium
   chicken broth
Onion
Garlic
Cider vinegar
Olive oil
Sugar substitute
Salt
Black peppercorns

Nutrition Facts:
Italian Roast Pork

Exchanges/Choices
4 Lean Meat

Calories	227
Calories from Fat	76
Total Fat	8 g
Saturated Fat	3 g
Cholesterol	97 mg
Sodium	71 mg
Carbohydrate	1 g
Dietary Fiber	0 g
Sugars	0 g
Protein	35 g

Italian Roast Pork

Preparation time: 25 minutes
Serves 2/Serving size: 1/2 recipe

1   medium clove garlic, crushed
1   Tbsp fresh sage, chopped (or 1/2 Tbsp dried)
3/4 lb pork tenderloin
1   tsp olive oil
    Salt and freshly ground black pepper

1. Preheat oven to 400°F. Line a baking tray with foil.

2. Mix garlic and sage together.

3. Remove fat from pork and cut nearly in half lengthwise. Do not cut all the way through. Open the pork like a book. With a sharp knife, make deep incisions in the pork and insert a little of the garlic-sage mixture in each incision.

4. Brush meat with oil and place on baking tray in the oven. Roast for 15 minutes or until a meat thermometer reads 160°F. Sprinkle with salt and pepper.

5. Slice and serve over the lentils.

Nutrition Facts:
Herbed Garlic Lentils

Exchanges/Choices
2 Starch
2 Vegetable
1 Lean Meat
1 Fat

Calories	276
Calories from Fat	71
Total Fat	8 g
Saturated Fat	1 g
Cholesterol	0 mg
Sodium	518 mg
Carbohydrate	39 g
Dietary Fiber	13 g
Sugars	12 g
Protein	16 g

Herbed Garlic Lentils
Preparation time: 25 minutes
Serves 2/Serving size: 1/2 recipe

- 1/2 cup dried lentils
- 2 cups fat-free reduced-sodium chicken broth
- 1 cup onion, sliced
- 2 medium cloves garlic, crushed
- 2 tsp cider vinegar
- 1 Tbsp olive oil
  Salt and freshly ground black pepper to taste
- 2 medium tomatoes, sliced

1. Place lentils in a strainer and discard any stones that you find. Rinse and drain.

2. Place a medium-size saucepan over medium-high heat and add chicken broth. Bring to a rolling boil.

3. Pour lentils into the pot slowly so that the water does not stop boiling. Add the onion and garlic. Reduce heat to medium, cover, and simmer 20 minutes. Check after 15 minutes to see if the pan is dry. Add 1/4 cup water if needed. If there is too much liquid, remove lid and boil to evaporate.

4. Remove from heat and add vinegar, oil, salt, and pepper. Toss well.

5. Place on individual plates with the sliced pork arranged on top and sliced tomatoes on the side.

Nutrition Facts:
Grapefruit with Toasted Pine Nuts

Exchanges/Choices
1 Fruit
1 Fat

Calories	107
Calories from Fat	48
Total Fat	5 g
Saturated Fat	1 g
Cholesterol	0 mg
Sodium	0 mg
Carbohydrate	15 g
Dietary Fiber	2 g
Sugars	11 g
Protein	3 g

Grapefruit with Toasted Pine Nuts
Preparation time: 5 minutes
Serves 2/Serving size: 1/2 recipe

- 1 large grapefruit, peeled and sliced
- 2 Tbsp pine nuts
  Sugar substitute equivalent to 2 tsp sugar

1. Divide grapefruit slices between two dessert plates.

2. Toast pine nuts in a toaster oven or in a small skillet until slightly golden, about 1 minute.

3. Sprinkle sugar substitute and pine nuts over grapefruit.

Baked Shrimp

with Roman Spinach and Orzo and Mocha-Cream Iced Soda

This Baked Shrimp takes less than 15 minutes to make. It is a quick, light dinner using a cooking method that leaves the shrimp juicy, firm, and flavorful.

Helpful Hints

◆ Orzo is small rice-shaped pasta. You can use any type of small pasta or leftover pasta pieces in this recipe.

◆ Buy good-quality Parmesan cheese and ask the market to grate it for you or chop it in the food processor. Freeze extra for quick use. You can spoon out what you need and leave the rest frozen.

◆ Buy shelled shrimp or ask for the shrimp to be shelled when you buy it. Many supermarkets will do this for a small fee. The time saved is worth the slightly higher cost.

◆ Make dessert at the last minute so the soda is fizzy and foamy.

Countdown

◆ Place water for orzo on to boil

◆ Preheat oven

◆ Boil orzo

◆ Make shrimp

◆ Finish orzo

◆ Make dessert

SHOPPING LIST

PRODUCE
1 10-oz package washed ready-to-eat spinach

SEAFOOD
1/2 lb large peeled and deveined shrimp

GROCERY
1 small bottle dry white wine
8 oz soda water (seltzer)
1 small package orzo
1 small carton low-fat chocolate frozen yogurt

STAPLES
Parmesan cheese
Plain bread crumbs
Raisins
Decaffeinated instant coffee
Sugar substitute
Olive oil
Salt
Black peppercorns

Nutrition Facts:
Baked Shrimp

Exchanges/Choices
1/2 Starch
3 Lean Meat
1/2 Fat

Calories	168
Calories from Fat	48
Total Fat	5 g
Saturated Fat	1 g
Cholesterol	179 mg
Sodium	302 mg
Carbohydrate	5 g
Dietary Fiber	0 g
Sugars	1 g
Protein	22 g

Baked Shrimp

Preparation time: 15 minutes
Serves 2/Serving size: 1/2 recipe

- 1/2 lb large peeled and deveined shrimp
- 2 Tbsp plain bread crumbs
- Salt and freshly ground black pepper to taste
- 1 tsp olive oil
- 1/4 cup dry white wine
- 2 Tbsp grated Parmesan cheese

1. Preheat oven to 350°F.

2. Place shrimp in a small baking dish just large enough to hold them in one layer. Sprinkle with bread crumbs, salt, and pepper. Toss to make sure shrimp is coated with bread crumbs.

3. Drizzle oil over shrimp.

4. Pour wine into baking dish and bake for 10 minutes.

5. Remove from oven and turn on broiler. Sprinkle top with Parmesan cheese and place under broiler for 1 minute. Watch carefully—it will brown quickly!

6. Remove from broiler and serve with orzo and spinach.

Roman Spinach and Orzo

Preparation time: 15 minutes
Serves 2/Serving size: 1/2 recipe

1/2	cup orzo
10	oz washed ready-to-eat spinach
1/4	cup water
2	Tbsp raisins
2	tsp olive oil
	Salt and freshly ground black pepper to taste

1. Place a medium-size saucepan 3/4 full of water on to boil for orzo. When water comes to a boil, add orzo and boil 9–10 minutes. Drain and set orzo aside.

2. In the same saucepan, place spinach and water and cover. Cook over medium-high heat 3–4 minutes.

3. Stir in raisins, oil, and orzo.

4. Add salt and pepper and serve.

Nutrition Facts:
Roman Spinach and Orzo

Exchanges/Choices
2 Starch
1/2 Fruit
1 Vegetable
1 Fat

Calories	258
Calories from Fat	51
Total Fat	6 g
Saturated Fat	1 g
Cholesterol	0 mg
Sodium	114 mg
Carbohydrate	43 g
Dietary Fiber	6 g
Sugars	8 g
Protein	10 g

Mocha-Cream Iced Soda

Preparation time: 5 minutes
Serves 2/Serving size: 1/2 recipe

2	tsp instant decaffeinated coffee
1/2	cup hot water
	Sugar substitute equivalent to 2 tsp
4–5	ice cubes
1/2	cup low-fat chocolate frozen yogurt
8	oz plain soda water (seltzer)

1. Dissolve coffee in hot water.

2. Add sugar substitute and place in refrigerator or freezer to cool for a few minutes.

3. Place ice cubes and coffee mixture in two tall glasses.

4. Add frozen yogurt to each glass.

5. Pour soda water over frozen yogurt.

6. Serve with a straw and a long spoon.

Nutrition Facts:
Mocha-Cream Iced Soda

Exchanges/Choices
1 Carbohydrate

Calories	60
Calories from Fat	7
Total Fat	1 g
Saturated Fat	1 g
Cholesterol	4 mg
Sodium	50 mg
Carbohydrate	12 g
Dietary Fiber	1 g
Sugars	7 g
Protein	2 g

Chinese Steamed Fish

with Spinach and Noodles and Grapefruit with Grand Marnier

Juicy, moist, flavorful fish is a Chinese specialty. The Chinese method of steaming helps preserve the fish's delicate flavor and texture. Chinese chefs add flavor with their sauces and vegetables.

This fish is steamed on a dinner plate to hold the juices and sauce. You will need a pot that is wide enough to hold the plate. I find the easiest thing to do at home is place a vegetable steamer opened as flat as possible in a large pot. The plate can then sit on the steamer. Or, you can place the plate on a meat rack in a roasting pan that has a cover.

Helpful Hints

♦ You can use yellowtail snapper or sole instead of flounder in this recipe.

♦ Look for fresh Chinese noodles in the produce department of most supermarkets, or use angel hair pasta instead.

♦ If you prefer, you can use orange juice instead of Grand Marnier or another orange-flavored liqueur for the dessert.

♦ Chopped fresh ginger is used in both recipes, so chop it all at once and divide accordingly.

♦ A quick way to chop ginger is to peel it, cut it into chunks, and press it through a garlic press with large holes. Press ginger over food or a bowl to catch its juices. The ginger pulp will not go through a small garlic press. Just the juice is enough to flavor the dish.

Countdown

♦ Place water for Chinese noodles on to boil

♦ Make dessert

♦ Steam fish

♦ Make noodles

SHOPPING LIST

PRODUCE
1 small package button mushrooms (2 oz)
1 bunch scallions
1 small piece fresh ginger
1 10-oz bag washed ready-to-eat fresh spinach
1 large grapefruit
1 package fresh Chinese egg noodles

SEAFOOD
3/4 lb flounder fillet

GROCERY
1 small bottle dry sherry
1 small bottle Grand Marnier

STAPLES

Garlic
Lite soy sauce
Sesame oil
Salt
Black peppercorns

Nutrition Facts:
Chinese Steamed Fish

Exchanges/Choices
1/2 Fruit
5 Lean Meat
1/2 Fat

Calories	217
Calories from Fat	39
Total Fat	4 g
Saturated Fat	0 g
Cholesterol	89 mg
Sodium	249 mg
Carbohydrate	6 g
Dietary Fiber	1 g
Sugars	3 g
Protein	33 g

Chinese Steamed Fish

Preparation time: 10 minutes
Serves 2/Serving size: 1/2 recipe

3/4 lb flounder fillet
1 cup thinly sliced button mushrooms
4 scallions, thinly sliced
2 tsp chopped fresh ginger
3 Tbsp dry sherry
1 tsp lite soy sauce
1 tsp sesame oil

1. Rinse fish, pat dry, and place on plate that will fit in a steamer.

2. Place vegetables and ginger on top of fish.

3. Mix sherry, soy sauce, and oil together. Pour over fish.

4. Bring water in steamer to a boil, place plate on a steaming rack, and cover.

5. Steam vigorously for 5 minutes.

6. Remove from steamer and serve.

Nutrition Facts:
Spinach and Noodles

Exchanges/Choices
2 Starch
1 Vegetable
1 Fat

Calories	230
Calories from Fat	53
Total Fat	6 g
Saturated Fat	0 g
Cholesterol	54 mg
Sodium	831 mg
Carbohydrate	37 g
Dietary Fiber	6 g
Sugars	3 g
Protein	13 g

Spinach and Noodles
Preparation time: 10 minutes
Serves 2/Serving size: 1/2 recipe

1/4 lb fresh Chinese egg noodles
1 tsp sesame oil
1 tsp chopped fresh ginger
1 medium clove garlic, crushed
1 10-oz bag washed ready-to-eat spinach
2 Tbsp lite soy sauce
Salt and freshly ground black pepper to taste

1. Bring a saucepan half full of water to a boil. Add noodles and simmer 3 minutes or until soft but not sticky. Drain.

2. Heat oil in the same pan and add ginger and garlic. Let cook a few seconds and add spinach.

3. Pour soy sauce over spinach.

4. Add noodles and toss with the spinach, breaking up the spinach leaves with the side of the spoon. Add salt and pepper.

5. Spoon onto plate with fish and serve.

Nutrition Facts:
Grapefruit with
Grand Marnier

Exchanges/Choices
1/2 Fruit

Calories	89
Calories from Fat	1
Total Fat	0 g
Saturated Fat	0 g
Cholesterol	0 mg
Sodium	1 mg
Carbohydrate	15 g
Dietary Fiber	1 g
Sugars	5 g
Protein	1 g

Grapefruit with Grand Marnier
1. Serve 1/2 large grapefruit sprinkled with 1 tablespoon Grand Marnier (or other orange-flavored liqueur) per person.

Wok-Flashed Shrimp

with Lemon Basmati Rice and Oranges

Peppery, stir-fried shrimp served over a bed of tart, lemony rice makes a delicious Chinese dinner. Basmati rice has a fragrant aroma and smells like popcorn when it's cooking. I've added peas to the rice because they're quick and easy to use, but any type of green vegetable will work fine.

Helpful Hints

◆ You can use any type of white rice.

◆ Buy shelled shrimp or ask for the shrimp to be shelled when you buy it. Many supermarkets will do this for a small fee. The time saved is worth the slightly higher cost.

◆ Chopped fresh ginger is used in both recipes, so chop it all at once and divide accordingly.

Countdown

◆ Start rice

◆ Prepare shrimp ingredients

◆ Finish rice

◆ Stir-fry shrimp

SHOPPING LIST

PRODUCE
1 small piece fresh ginger
2 small oranges

SEAFOOD
3/4 lb large shelled shrimp

GROCERY
1 package basmati rice
1 package frozen tiny peas

STAPLES

Lemon
Garlic
Cornstarch
Canola oil
Fat-free reduced-sodium
   chicken broth
Salt
Black peppercorns

Wok-Flashed Shrimp

Nutrition Facts:
Wok-Flashed Shrimp

Exchanges/Choices
1/2 Carbohydrate
4 Lean Meat
1 Fat

Calories	230
Calories from Fat	82
Total Fat	9 g
Saturated Fat	0 g
Cholesterol	201 mg
Sodium	781 mg
Carbohydrate	9 g
Dietary Fiber	1 g
Sugars	3 g
Protein	27 g

Preparation time: 10 minutes
Serves 2/Serving size: 1/2 recipe

- 3/4 lb large shrimp, peeled and deveined
- 1 Tbsp cornstarch
- 1/2 tsp salt
- 1/4 tsp freshly ground black pepper
- 1 Tbsp diced fresh ginger (or 1 tsp ground ginger)
- 1 Tbsp canola oil
- 5 cloves garlic, crushed

1. Place shrimp in a bowl of water to soak while you prepare the other ingredients. Mix cornstarch, salt, black pepper, and ginger together in a medium-size bowl.

2. Remove shrimp from water, pat dry with a paper towel, and add to the cornstarch mixture. Toss well to make sure all of the shrimp are covered with the mixture.

3. Heat oil in a wok or skillet over high heat. When oil is smoking, add shrimp and garlic. Stir-fry 4–5 minutes.

4. Serve shrimp over rice.

Nutrition Facts:
Lemon Basmati Rice

Exchanges/Choices
3 1/2 Starch
1 Fat

Calories	313
Calories from Fat	65
Total Fat	**7 g**
Saturated Fat	0 g
Cholesterol	**0 mg**
Sodium	**323 mg**
Carbohydrate	**54 g**
Dietary Fiber	6 g
Sugars	5 g
Protein	**9 g**

Lemon Basmati Rice
Preparation time: 20 minutes
Serves 2/Serving size: 1/2 recipe

    1   Tbsp canola oil
  1/2   cup basmati rice
    2   Tbsp fresh lemon juice
    1   1/4-inch piece fresh ginger
    1   cup fat-free reduced-sodium chicken broth
    1   cup frozen peas
        Salt and freshly ground black pepper to taste

1. Heat oil in a small nonstick skillet over medium heat. Add rice and stir 1 minute.

2. Add lemon juice, ginger, and chicken broth. Bring to a boil, cover, and simmer 10 minutes. Add peas, cover, and cook 5 minutes.

3. Remove ginger, add salt and pepper, and serve.

Nutrition Facts:
Orange

Exchanges/Choices
1 Fruit

Calories	70
Calories from Fat	0
Total Fat	**0 g**
Saturated Fat	0 g
Cholesterol	**0 mg**
Sodium	**0 mg**
Carbohydrate	**18 g**
Dietary Fiber	4 g
Sugars	14 g
Protein	**1 g**

Oranges
1. Serve one small orange per person.

Italian Fish Soup

with Romaine and Bean Salad and Ginger Apples and Bananas

Italian Fish Soup (Zuppa di Pesce) is a perfect soup to brighten any table. Every coastal town in Italy has its own fish soup based on the types of fish found in that area. This is an aromatic soup that is a meal in itself. For this quick meal, one type of fish and some shellfish work well. Of course, the fresher the fish the better. I have chosen grouper because it is a firm fish that cooks well and is readily available. Any type of non-oily fish that will hold its shape when cooked can be used.

Helpful Hints

♦ Any type of beans can be used.

♦ The dessert is made in a microwave oven which takes only 2 minutes. A conventional oven can be used. Bake at 400°F for 10 minutes.

Countdown

♦ Start fish soup

♦ Make salad

♦ Make dessert

♦ Finish soup

SHOPPING LIST

DAIRY
1 package light buttery spread
   (such as Smart Balance)

PRODUCE
1 small bunch parsley
1/2 lb plum tomatoes
1 medium banana
1 10-oz bag washed ready-to-eat
   Romaine lettuce

SEAFOOD
1/2 lb grouper
1/2 lb clams

GROCERY
1 tin anchovy fillets
1 small bottle dry white wine
1 bottle clam juice
1 small package gingersnaps
1 small loaf country-style
   whole-grain bread
1 small can cannellini beans

STAPLES

Apple	Oil and vinegar dressing
Olive oil	Onion
Carrots	Celery
Garlic	Hot pepper sauce
Salt	Black peppercorns

Nutrition Facts:
Italian Fish Soup

Exchanges/Choices
1 Starch
3 Vegetables
5 Lean Meat
1/2 Fat

Calories	405
Calories from Fat	70
Total Fat	8 g
Saturated Fat	1.3 g
Cholesterol	85 mg
Sodium	630 mg
Carbohydrate	31 g
Dietary Fiber	6 g
Sugars	13 g
Protein	45 g

Italian Fish Soup
(*Zuppa Di Pesce*)

Preparation time: 20 minutes
Serve: 2/Serving size: 1/2 recipe

2	tsp olive oil
1	cup onion, sliced
1	celery stalk, sliced (about 1/2 cup)
1	carrot, sliced (about 1/2 cup)
1	clove garlic, crushed
1	anchovy fillet
	Several parsley sprigs (about 1/4 cup)
1	cup dry white wine
1	cup clam juice
1/2	lb plum tomatoes, chopped (about 1 1/2 cups)
1/2	lb clams (yields 1/4 lb clam meat)
1/2	lb grouper, cut into 3-inch pieces
2	slices country-style whole-grain bread
	Salt and freshly ground pepper
	Hot pepper sauce

1. Heat olive oil in a large saucepan over medium-high heat. Add onion, celery, carrot, garlic, anchovy, and parsley. Gently sauté the ingredients until the onion turns a golden color, about 5 minutes. Do not let the vegetables burn.

2. Carefully stir in wine, clam juice, and tomatoes. Simmer gently for 5 minutes to reduce the liquid.

3. Scrub clam shells. Add clams in their shells and grouper. Season with salt and pepper to taste.

4. Bring the soup to a simmer, lower the heat and cook, gently, for 5 minutes. Check the seasoning and add more, if necessary. Serve in large soup bowls with bread on the side, passing the hot pepper sauce to be used as desired.

Nutrition Facts:
Romaine and Bean Salad

Exchanges/Choices
1 Carbohydrate
1 1/2 Fat

Calories	145
Calories from Fat	70
Total Fat	8 g
Saturated Fat	1.3 g
Cholesterol	0 mg
Sodium	125 mg
Carbohydrate	13 g
Dietary Fiber	4 g
Sugars	1 g
Protein	5 g

Romaine and Bean Salad

Preparation time: 2 minutes
Serves: 2/Serving size: 1/2 recipe

1/2 10-oz bag washed ready-to-eat Romaine lettuce
1/2 cup cannellini beans, rinsed and drained
2 Tbsp oil and vinegar dressing

1. Place lettuce and beans in a salad bowl and toss with the dressing.

Nutrition Facts:
Ginger Apples
and Bananas

Exchanges/Choices
1 1/2 Fruit
1/2 Carbohydrate
1/2 Fat

Calories	155
Calories from Fat	30
Total Fat	3.5 g
Saturated Fat	0.9 g
Cholesterol	0 mg
Sodium	125 mg
Carbohydrate	32 g
Dietary Fiber	3 g
Sugars	16 g
Protein	2 g

Ginger Apples and Bananas

Preparation time: 5 minutes
Serves: 2/Serving size: 1/2 recipe

1 small apple, cored and cut into 1/2-inch cubes (1 cup)
1 medium banana, cut into 1/2-inch slices (3/4 cup)
2 tsp light buttery spread (such as Smart Balance)
4 gingersnaps, crumbled or broken into small pieces
2 ramekins or small oven-proof bowls about 3 × 1 × 3/4-inches deep

1. Divide apple and banana equally between two oven-proof bowls.

2. Break butter into small pieces and sprinkle on top of fruit.

3. Sprinkle gingersnap crumbs on top.

4. Microwave each one separately on high 1 minute.

Claudine's Tilapia

with Saffron Broccoli and Potatoes and Kiwis with Raspberry Sauce

Steamed broccoli and potatoes are delicious with the addition of saffron. This side dish is the perfect accompaniment to a sautéed fish fillet with scallion topping. Recently, I was visiting the home of television chef Jacques Pepin in Connecticut when their daughter Claudine called to ask how to add a little extra flavor to broccoli. Jacques's wife Gloria told her to steam it and toss it with oil infused with a little saffron. I think you'll agree: the result is delicious!

Helpful Hints

- You can use turmeric instead of saffron. The flavor will be different, but still delicious.
- Tilapia, also known as St. Peter's fish, is now being farm raised and is available in many supermarkets. It is a flaky white fish. You can substitute any type of non-oily fish in this recipe, such as snapper, sole, or flounder.
- You can use frozen raspberries for the dessert, but look for ones frozen without sugar syrup.
- If you don't have a steamer, make your own with a large saucepan and a colander. Place the potatoes and broccoli in a metal colander just large enough to sit on the top of the pan with the bottom above the water level.

Countdown

- Start vegetables
- Make dessert
- Sauté fish
- Finish vegetables

SHOPPING LIST

PRODUCE
3/4 lb yellow potatoes
3/4 lb broccoli florets
1 bunch scallions
2 kiwi fruits
1 small container raspberries

SEAFOOD
3/4 lb tilapia fillets (or other white fish fillet)

GROCERY
1 small package saffron threads

STAPLES
Lemon
Olive oil
Salt
Black peppercorns

Claudine's Tilapia

Nutrition Facts:
Claudine's Tilapia

Exchanges/Choices
5 Lean Meat
1 Fat

Calories	205
Calories from Fat	58
Total Fat	6 g
Saturated Fat	1 g
Cholesterol	89 mg
Sodium	148 mg
Carbohydrate	3 g
Dietary Fiber	1 g
Sugars	1 g
Protein	32 g

Preparation time: 10 minutes
Serves 2/Serving size: 1/2 recipe

3/4 lb tilapia or other white fish fillet
  2 tsp olive oil
    Salt and freshly ground black pepper to taste
  2 scallions, sliced
  1 lemon, cut into four wedges

1. Rinse fish and pat dry with a paper towel.

2. Heat oil in a nonstick skillet over medium-high heat. Add tilapia and sauté 3 minutes. Turn and sauté 3 minutes. Salt and pepper the cooked side.

3. Sprinkle with scallions, cover, and cook 1 minute.

4. Remove tilapia to two dinner plates and squeeze juice from two lemon wedges on top. Serve remaining lemon wedge on each plate.

Nutrition Facts:
Saffron Broccoli
and Potatoes

Exchanges/Choices	
2 Starch	
2 Vegetable	
1 Fat	

Calories	249
Calories from Fat	69
Total Fat	8 g
Saturated Fat	1 g
Cholesterol	0 mg
Sodium	52 mg
Carbohydrate	41 g
Dietary Fiber	8 g
Sugars	6 g
Protein	8 g

Saffron Broccoli and Potatoes

Preparation time: 15 minutes
Serves 2/Serving size: 1/2 recipe

- 3/4 lb yellow potatoes
- 3/4 lb broccoli florets
- 1 Tbsp olive oil
- 1/8 tsp saffron threads (8–10 threads)
  Salt and freshly ground black pepper to taste
- 1/2 cup hot water from steamer

1. Wash potatoes, do not peel, and cut into 1-inch pieces. Place in steaming basket with broccoli. Add 2 inches of water to the base of the steamer or saucepan and add the steaming basket. Cover pot and bring water to a boil. Steam 10 minutes.

2. Heat oil and saffron in a mixing bowl for 15 seconds in a microwave oven, or place bowl over steamer to warm oil and saffron. Add salt and pepper.

3. When potatoes and broccoli are ready, add 1/2 cup steaming water to the oil in the bowl. Add potatoes and broccoli and toss well.

Nutrition Facts:
Kiwis with
Raspberry Sauce

Exchanges/Choices	
1 1/2 Fruit	

Calories	87
Calories from Fat	7
Total Fat	1 g
Saturated Fat	0 g
Cholesterol	0 mg
Sodium	5 mg
Carbohydrate	21 g
Dietary Fiber	7 g
Sugars	13 g
Protein	1 g

Kiwis with Raspberry Sauce

Preparation time: 5 minutes
Serves 2/Serving size: 1/2 recipe

- 2 kiwi fruit
- 1 cup fresh raspberries
  Sugar substitute equivalent to 1 tsp sugar

1. Purée raspberries in a food processor, food mill, or through a sieve.

2. Add sugar substitute to the purée and spoon onto two dessert plates.

3. Peel and slice kiwis and arrange slices on top of purée.

Crisp Thai Snapper

with Island Salad and Plum-Glazed Figs

Fresh, sweet fish topped with a layer of mustard and golden, crisp, shredded potatoes was one of the dishes I tasted in Anguilla, one of the Eastern Caribbean's Leeward Islands. The fishermen go out in their homebuilt boats every day and bring their fresh catches to restaurants and islanders. A simple Thai sauce adds an Asian flavor to the dish.

Helpful Hints

◆ You can use any type of white fish.

◆ Use the grating blade of the food processor or a grater with large holes to shred the potato.

Countdown

◆ Make dessert

◆ Make snapper dressing

◆ Make salad

◆ Cook snapper

SHOPPING LIST

PRODUCE
1 small piece fresh ginger or
   1 jar ground ginger
1/4 lb shredded russet or
   Idaho potato
1 head Boston lettuce
4 small figs

SEAFOOD
3/4 lb yellowtail snapper or
   other light fish fillet

GROCERY
1 can hearts of palm
1 small jar low-sugar plum
   spreadable fruit

STAPLES

Lemon
Lite soy sauce
Dijon mustard
Sugar substitute
Olive oil
Oil and vinegar salad dressing
Salt
Black peppercorns

Crisp Thai Snapper

Nutrition Facts:
Crisp Thai Snapper

Exchanges/Choices
1 Starch
5 Lean Meat
1/2 Fat

Calories	280
Calories from Fat	67
Total Fat	**7 g**
Saturated Fat	1 g
Cholesterol	**61 mg**
Sodium	**1,046 mg**
Carbohydrate	**14 g**
Dietary Fiber	1 g
Sugars	4 g
Protein	**38 g**

Preparation time: 15 minutes
Serves 2/Serving size: 1/2 recipe

> 1 Tbsp lemon juice
> Sugar substitute equivalent to 1 tsp sugar
> 2 Tbsp lite soy sauce
> 1 tsp chopped ginger or 1/2 tsp dried ginger
> 3/4 lb yellowtail snapper or other light fish fillet, skin removed
> 2 Tbsp Dijon mustard
> 1/2 cup shredded russet or Idaho potato (1/4 lb needed)
> 2 tsp olive oil
> Salt and freshly ground black pepper to taste

1. In a small bowl, mix lemon juice, sugar substitute, soy sauce, and ginger together and set aside.

2. Rinse fish and pat dry with a paper towel. Spread mustard over one side of fish and place shredded potato on top. Pat potato down so that it is firmly in place.

3. Heat oil over medium-high heat in a nonstick skillet just large enough to hold the fish in one layer. Add fish, potato side up. Sauté 3 minutes. Gently turn fish over and cook 5 minutes to brown potatoes. Salt and pepper the cooked side. Lower heat if potatoes are browning too quickly.

4. Remove fish to individual dinner plates with potato side up. Salt and pepper the potato side. Add sauce from small bowl to the skillet. Warm sauce about 30 seconds and pour over fish.

Island Salad

Preparation time: 5 minutes
Serves 2/Serving size: 1/2 recipe

1/2 head Boston lettuce
  1 cup canned hearts of palm, drained and sliced
  2 Tbsp oil and vinegar salad dressing

1. Wash and dry lettuce and tear into bite-sized pieces. Place in salad bowl.

2. Add hearts of palm and dressing. Toss and serve with the fish.

Nutrition Facts:
Island Salad

Exchanges/Choices
1 Vegetable
2 Fat

Calories	113
Calories from Fat	79
Total Fat	**9 g**
Saturated Fat	1 g
Cholesterol	**0 mg**
Sodium	**480 mg**
Carbohydrate	**7 g**
Dietary Fiber	4 g
Sugars	3 g
Protein	**3 g**

Plum-Glazed Figs

Preparation time: 2 minutes
Serves 2/Serving size: 1/2 recipe

4 ripe fresh figs
2 Tbsp low-sugar plum spreadable fruit

1. Cut figs into quarters and divide between two small dessert plates.

2. Warm spread in a microwave oven on high for 10 seconds or in a saucepan for 30 seconds.

3. Spoon warm spread over fig quarters.

Nutrition Facts:
Plum-Glazed Figs

Exchanges/Choices
1 1/2 Fruit

Calories	99
Calories from Fat	3
Total Fat	**0 g**
Saturated Fat	0 g
Cholesterol	**0 mg**
Sodium	**12 mg**
Carbohydrate	**25 g**
Dietary Fiber	3 g
Sugars	12 g
Protein	**1 g**

Seafood Kabobs

with Brown Rice and Pear Custard

Kabobs with a mixture of seafood and colorful vegetables make a quick, flavorful dinner. I chose shrimp and scallops for their texture and flavor. Zucchini and yellow squash add color and crispness. These kabobs need only 5 minutes to cook. The pieces will be crisp outside and moist and tender inside.

Helpful Hints

◆ You can use any type of seafood chunks.

◆ Leave about 1/4 inch between the ingredients on the skewer to allow for even cooking.

◆ Make sure the grill is hot before cooking the kabobs, or use a hot broiler.

◆ I like to boil rice like pasta in a pot large enough to let the grains roll freely in the boiling water. This method yields fluffy rice every time.

◆ To save washing extra bowls, measure milk for dessert in a liquid measuring container and mix remaining ingredients in the same container.

Countdown

◆ Preheat oven

◆ Make rice

◆ Make dessert

◆ Marinate kabobs

◆ Preheat grill

◆ Grill kabobs

SHOPPING LIST

PRODUCE
1 lime
1 medium zucchini
1 bunch fresh dill
1 medium yellow squash
1 ripe pear

SEAFOOD
6 oz large shelled shrimp
6 oz large sea scallops

GROCERY
1 small package walnut pieces

STAPLES
Garlic
Fat-free milk
Eggs
Olive oil
Sugar substitute
Vanilla extract
Quick-cooking brown rice
Salt
Black peppercorns

Nutrition Facts:
Seafood Kabobs

Exchanges/Choices
2 Vegetable
4 Lean Meat
1/2 Fat

Calories	224
Calories from Fat	42
Total Fat	5 g
Saturated Fat	0 g
Cholesterol	157 mg
Sodium	314 mg
Carbohydrate	12 g
Dietary Fiber	4 g
Sugars	7 g
Protein	34 g

Seafood Kabobs

Preparation time: 25 minutes
Serves 2/Serving size: 1/2 recipe

- 2 Tbsp lime juice
- 1 Tbsp olive oil
- 1 clove garlic, crushed
- 1/8 tsp salt
- 1/4 tsp freshly ground black pepper
- 2 tsp fresh snipped dill
- 12 large shelled deveined shrimp (6 oz)
- 7 large sea scallops (6 oz)
- 1 medium zucchini cut into 1-inch pieces (2 cups)
- 1 medium yellow squash cut into 1-inch pieces (2 cups)

1. Preheat grill or broiler.

2. Mix lime juice, olive oil, garlic, salt, pepper, and dill together.

3. Add shrimp, scallops, and vegetables and set aside to marinate for 15 minutes. Turn once during this time.

4. Alternate vegetables, shrimp, and scallops on four skewers. Grill or broil 3–4 inches from the heat source for 2 1/2 minutes per side. Do not overcook the fish. Sprinkle with salt and pepper.

5. Place skewers on two dinner plates or remove seafood and vegetables from skewers onto two plates and serve.

Nutrition Facts:
Brown Rice

Exchanges/Choices
2 1/2 Starch
1/2 Fat

Calories	210
Calories from Fat	54
Total Fat	6 g
Saturated Fat	1 g
Cholesterol	0 mg
Sodium	3 mg
Carbohydrate	35 g
Dietary Fiber	2 g
Sugars	0 g
Protein	5 g

Brown Rice
Preparation time: 35 minutes
Serves 2/Serving size: 1/2 recipe

- 1/2 cup quick-cooking brown rice
- 2 tsp olive oil
- Salt and freshly ground black pepper to taste

1. Fill a medium saucepan halfway with cold water and add rice. Bring water to a boil and gently boil rice for about 30 minutes. Test a few grains to see if they are cooked through but still firm.

2. Drain, leaving a little water on the rice. With a fork, stir in oil, salt, and pepper.

Nutrition Facts:
Pear Custard

Exchanges/Choices
1 Carbohydrate
1 Fat

Calories	135
Calories from Fat	47
Total Fat	5 g
Saturated Fat	1 g
Cholesterol	108 mg
Sodium	64 mg
Carbohydrate	17 g
Dietary Fiber	2 g
Sugars	13 g
Protein	6 g

Pear Custard
Preparation time: 35 minutes
Serves 2/Serving size: 1/2 recipe

- 1 ripe pear, peeled, cored, and cut into 1-inch pieces (1 cup)
- 1/2 cup fat-free milk
- Sugar substitute equivalent to 1/2 tsp sugar
- 1/2 tsp vanilla extract
- 1 egg
- 1 Tbsp walnut pieces

1. Preheat oven to 350°F.

2. Place pear pieces in two ramekins or small oven-proof bowls about 3 × 1 3/4 inches deep. Mix fat-free milk, sugar substitute, vanilla extract, and egg together and pour on top of pears.

3. Sprinkle walnuts on top and bake 30 minutes or until custard is firm.

4. Remove from oven, allow to cool a few minutes, and serve.

Sautéed Scallops

with Saffron Vegetable Pilaf and Mocha Froth

Sweet, tender scallops need very little cooking. In fact, to remain delicate and flavorful, they should be cooked only a few minutes over high heat in a skillet large enough to hold them in one layer without touching. The result will be a crusty coating while the inside remains juicy.

Helpful Hints

◆ Buy good quality Parmesan cheese and ask the market to grate it for you or chop it in the food processor. Freeze extra for quick use. You can quickly spoon out what you need and leave the rest frozen.

◆ Bijol or turmeric can be substituted for saffron. Although the flavor will be altered, the dish is still very good.

◆ Small bay scallops can be used instead of the large sea scallops. Reduce cooking time to 1 minute per side.

Countdown

◆ Start pilaf

◆ Make scallops

◆ Finish pilaf

◆ Make dessert just before serving

SHOPPING LIST

PRODUCE
1 small package portobello
    mushrooms (1 oz needed)

DAIRY
1 small carton light cream
1 small piece Parmesan cheese

FISH
3/4 lb large scallops

GROCERY
1 small package saffron threads
1 small bottle dry vermouth
1 small package frozen peas
1 small package frozen chopped onion

STAPLES

Olive oil
Flour
Long-grain white rice
Decaffeinated instant coffee
Fat-free milk
Sugar substitute
Fat-free reduced-sodium chicken broth
Salt

Nutrition Facts:
Sautéed Scallops

Exchanges/Choices
4 Lean Meat
   (1/2 alcohol equivalent)

Calories	250
Calories from Fat	55
Total Fat	6 g
Saturated Fat	1 g
Cholesterol	70 mg
Sodium	475 mg
Carbohydrate	4 g
Dietary Fiber	0 g
Sugars	2 g
Protein	31 g

Sautéed Scallops

Preparation time: 10 minutes
Serves: 2/Serving size: 1/2 recipe

  2 tsp olive oil
3/4 lb large scallops
1/2 Tbsp flour
1/2 cup dry vermouth
1/2 cup fat-free, reduced-sodium chicken broth
  1 Tbsp light cream
    Salt and fresh ground black pepper

1. Heat oil in a nonstick skillet over medium-high heat. Add scallops and sauté 2 1/2 minutes on each side.

2. Remove scallops to a plate and add flour to pan.

3. Add vermouth to the pan, raise the heat to high, and reduce the liquid by half, about 1 minute. Add chicken broth and reduce by half again, about 1 minute. Remove from heat and stir in the cream. Add salt and pepper to taste.

4. Return scallops to the pan just to warm through, about 1/2 minute, and serve.

Nutrition Facts:
Saffron Vegetable Pilaf

Exchanges/Choices
3 Starch
1 Vegetable
1 Fat

Calories	305
Calories from Fat	40
Total Fat	4.5 g
Saturated Fat	1 g
Cholesterol	5 mg
Sodium	370 mg
Carbohydrate	54 g
Dietary Fiber	6 g
Sugars	7 g
Protein	12 g

Saffron Vegetable Pilaf

Preparation time: 20 minutes
Serves: 2/Serving size: 1/2 recipe

- 1 tsp olive oil
- 1/2 cup frozen chopped onion
- 1/2 cup portobello mushrooms, sliced
- 1/2 cup long-grain white rice
- 1 cup fat-free reduced-sodium chicken broth
- 1/4 tsp saffron threads
- 1 cup frozen peas
  Salt and fresh ground black pepper
- 2 Tbsp freshly grated Parmesan cheese

1. Heat olive oil in a nonstick skillet over medium-high heat. Add onion and mushrooms. Sauté 3 minutes.

2. Add rice and sauté 1 minute.

3. Add chicken broth and saffron.

4. Bring liquid to a simmer, cover with a lid, and cook 10 minutes. Add peas and continue to simmer, covered, 3 minutes. Liquid should be absorbed and rice cooked through. Simmer a few more minutes if needed.

5. Add salt and pepper to taste, sprinkle with Parmesan cheese, and serve with scallops.

Nutrition Facts:
Coffee Froth

Exchanges/Choices
1 Free Food

Calories	25
Calories from Fat	0
Total Fat	0 g
Saturated Fat	0 g
Cholesterol	0 mg
Sodium	40 mg
Carbohydrate	4 g
Dietary Fiber	0 g
Sugars	3 g
Protein	2 g

Coffee Froth

Preparation time: 5 minutes
Serves: 2/Serving size: 1/2 recipe

- 1 cup boiling water
- 2 tsp instant decaffeinated coffee
  Sugar substitute equivalent to 2 tsp sugar
- 1/2 cup fat-free milk
- 10 ice cubes

1. Pour boiling water into a blender and add coffee and sugar substitute.

2. Blend several seconds and add the milk and ice cubes. Blend until thick, about 1 minute.

3. Pour into tall glasses and serve with a straw and long spoon.

Shrimp Creole

with Brown Rice and Carambola Cooler

Fresh shrimp in a spicy tomato sauce is a classic New Orleans dish. Carambola Cooler, a refreshing tropical drink, provides a satisfying conclusion to the meal.

Helpful Hints

◆ Buy shelled shrimp or ask for the shrimp to be shelled when you buy it. Supermarkets will do this for you for a small fee. The time saved is worth the slightly higher cost.

◆ Buy tomato paste in a tube. You can use a small amount and store the rest of the tube in the refrigerator until you need it again.

◆ You can use any hot pepper sauce, in any quantity you can stand!

◆ Carambolas are also called star fruit. They are usually available from August to mid-February. Use strawberries as a substitute.

Countdown

◆ Purée carambola and refrigerate

◆ Make rice

◆ Make shrimp

◆ Assemble dessert

SHOPPING LIST

PRODUCE
1 medium green pepper
2 medium tomatoes
1/2 lb ripe carambolas
　　(2 medium or 5 small)

SEAFOOD
3/4 lb medium peeled and
　　deveined shrimp

GROCERY
1 can or tube tomato paste
1 small bottle soda water (seltzer)

STAPLES

Onion
Garlic
Quick-cooking brown rice
Canola oil
Worcestershire sauce
Hot pepper sauce
Sugar substitute
Salt
Black peppercorns

Nutrition Facts:
Shrimp Creole

Exchanges/Choices
3 Vegetable
4 Lean Meat
1 1/2 Fat

Calories	277
Calories from Fat	81
Total Fat	9 g
Saturated Fat	0 g
Cholesterol	261 mg
Sodium	385 mg
Carbohydrate	19 g
Dietary Fiber	4 g
Sugars	11 g
Protein	31 g

Shrimp Creole

Preparation time: 20 minutes
Serves 2/Serving size: 1/2 recipe

- 1 Tbsp canola oil
- 1 cup onion, sliced
- 1 cup green pepper, sliced
- 2 medium cloves garlic, crushed
- 2 cups diced tomatoes
- 1/2 Tbsp tomato paste
- 2 Tbsp water
- 1/2 Tbsp Worcestershire sauce
- 1 tsp hot pepper sauce
- 3/4 lb medium peeled and deveined shrimp

1. Heat oil in medium-size nonstick skillet over medium-high heat. Add onion, green pepper, and garlic and sauté 3 minutes.

2. Add tomatoes and sauté another 5 minutes.

3. Mix tomato paste with water and add to skillet along with Worcestershire and hot pepper sauce. Cook 1 minute.

4. Add shrimp and sauté 2–3 minutes.

5. To serve, spoon shrimp and sauce over rice.

Brown Rice

Preparation time: 35 minutes
Serves 2/Serving size: 1/2 recipe

- 1/2 cup quick-cooking brown rice
- 2 tsp canola oil
  Salt and freshly ground black pepper to taste

1. Fill a large saucepan 3/4 full of water, bring to a boil, and add rice.

2. Gently boil rice according to package instructions. Test a few grains to see if they are cooked through but still firm.

3. Strain into a colander, leaving a little water on the rice.

4. Add oil, salt, and pepper.

Nutrition Facts:
Brown Rice

Exchanges/Choices
2 1/2 Starch
1/2 Fat

Calories	210
Calories from Fat	54
Total Fat	6 g
Saturated Fat	1 g
Cholesterol	0 mg
Sodium	3 mg
Carbohydrate	35 g
Dietary Fiber	2 g
Sugars	0 g
Protein	5 g

Carambola Cooler

Preparation time: 5 minutes
Serves 2/Serving size: 1/2 recipe

- 1/2 lb ripe carambolas (2 medium or 5 small; 2 cups chunks yield 1/2 cup juice)
- 2 tsp sugar substitute
- 1/2 cup soda water (seltzer)
- 4 ice cubes

1. Wash carambola and slice two stars from the center of the largest fruit. Set aside for garnish.

2. Cut remaining fruit into large chunks. Place in food processor with sugar substitute and process 2 minutes or until fruit is turned into a pulpy juice. Strain into glass, being sure to press as much juice as possible from the pulp. Place in refrigerator until needed or up to 8 hours.

3. When ready, add soda water and ice cubes to the glasses.

4. Cut a slit halfway through each reserved star and stick it on the side of the glass as a garnish. Serve immediately.

Nutrition Facts:
Carambola Cooler

Exchanges/Choices
1 1/2 Fruit

Calories	36
Calories from Fat	3
Total Fat	0 g
Saturated Fat	0 g
Cholesterol	0 mg
Sodium	14 mg
Carbohydrate	8 g
Dietary Fiber	3 g
Sugars	6 g
Protein	1 g

Herb-Crusted Mahi-Mahi

with Vegetable Brown Rice and Apricot-Glazed Pears

When fish is really fresh, it needs only a few minutes to cook. Add fresh herbs and you have a quick, delicious meal.

Helpful Hints

◆ You can use any type of non-oily fish fillet in this recipe. Count 10 minutes cooking time for each inch of thickness. To check for doneness, stick the point of a knife into the flesh. If the flesh is opaque, it is ready.

◆ You can use green beans, zucchini, or any other green vegetable instead of broccoli.

◆ The dessert is best with any type of ripe pear, but it can be made with semi-ripe ones. Add sugar substitute equivalent to 1 tsp to the lemon juice if pears are not fully ripe.

Countdown

◆ Make rice

◆ Preheat broiler

◆ Broil fish

◆ Make dessert

SHOPPING LIST

PRODUCE
1 bunch parsley
1/2 lb broccoli florets
2 ripe pears

DAIRY
1 carton fat-free plain yogurt

SEAFOOD
3/4 lb mahi-mahi fillets

GROCERY
1 small package pine nuts
1 small jar low-sugar apricot spread

STAPLES

Lemon
Olive oil cooking spray
Olive oil
Butter
Quick-cooking brown rice
Salt
Black peppercorns

Herb-Crusted Mahi-Mahi

Nutrition Facts:
Herb-Crusted Mahi-Mahi

Exchanges/Choices
5 Lean Meat
1 1/2 Fat

Calories	247
Calories from Fat	98
Total Fat	11 g
Saturated Fat	2 g
Cholesterol	131 mg
Sodium	162 mg
Carbohydrate	2 g
Dietary Fiber	1 g
Sugars	0 g
Protein	36 g

Preparation time: 15 minutes
Serves 2/Serving size: 1/2 recipe

> Olive oil cooking spray
> 3/4 lb mahi-mahi fillets
> 2 tsp olive oil
> 2 Tbsp pine nuts
> 1/4 cup chopped fresh parsley
> Salt and freshly ground black pepper to taste

1. Preheat broiler.

2. Line a baking sheet with foil and spray it with cooking spray. Place mahi-mahi on sheet and spray it with cooking spray.

3. Place sheet under broiler about 3–4 inches from heat source. Broil 5 minutes on each side for a piece 1-inch thick.

4. Heat oil in a small skillet on medium heat and add pine nuts. Sauté 1 minute or until pine nuts start to turn golden. Remove from heat and toss with parsley.

5. Remove mahi-mahi and divide between two dinner plates. Add salt and pepper. Spoon pine nuts and herbs on top.

Nutrition Facts:
Vegetable Brown Rice

Exchanges/Choices
2 1/2 Starch

Calories	212
Calories from Fat	14
Total Fat	2 g
Saturated Fat	0 g
Cholesterol	1 mg
Sodium	62 mg
Carbohydrate	41 g
Dietary Fiber	2 g
Sugars	5 g
Protein	9 g

Vegetable Brown Rice

Preparation time: 35 minutes
Serves 2/Serving size: 1/2 recipe

1 1/2 cups water
1/2 cup quick-cooking 30-minute brown rice
1/2 lb broccoli florets
     Salt and freshly ground black pepper to taste
1/2 cup fat-free plain yogurt

1. Place water in a medium-size saucepan over high heat. Add rice and bring to a boil.

2. Reduce heat to medium and cover. Simmer 25 minutes.

3. Add broccoli and continue to cook, covered, 5 minutes. All of the water should be absorbed and the rice cooked through.

4. Add salt, pepper, and yogurt. Toss well.

Nutrition Facts:
Apricot-Glazed Pears

Exchanges/Choices
2 Fruit
1/2 Fat

Calories	128
Calories from Fat	22
Total Fat	2 g
Saturated Fat	1 g
Cholesterol	5 mg
Sodium	34 mg
Carbohydrate	28 g
Dietary Fiber	3 g
Sugars	22 g
Protein	1 g

Apricot-Glazed Pears

Preparation time: 10 minutes
Serves 2/Serving size: 1/2 recipe

2 ripe pears
1 tsp butter
2 Tbsp lemon juice
2 Tbsp low-sugar apricot spread

1. Core and slice pears.

2. Heat butter in a medium nonstick skillet over medium heat and add the pear slices. Sauté 1 minute.

3. Mix lemon juice with apricot spread and add to skillet. Toss to coat pears.

4. Cover skillet and cook 5 minutes or until pears are soft. Divide between two dinner plates and pour juice on top.

Key West Shrimp

with Quick Coleslaw and Strawberries and Cream Angel Food Cake

Succulent, fresh pink shrimp are a trademark of the Florida Keys. This is a never-fail recipe for cooking shrimp. Use it for other recipes that use shrimp.

Shredded, ready-to-eat cabbage and carrots are found in the produce section of the supermarket. They make preparing homemade coleslaw a breeze. I prefer to add my own dressing to it. Bought coleslaw is usually dripping in mayonnaise and sometimes has added sugar.

Helpful Hints

◆ Any type of shrimp can be used.

◆ Lemon or lime juice can be used instead of bottled key lime juice.

◆ Buy shelled shrimp or ask for the shrimp to be shelled when you buy it. Many supermarkets will do this for a small fee. I find the slightly higher cost is worth the time saved.

Countdown

◆ Make coleslaw and let marinate while preparing shrimp and sauce

◆ Boil shrimp

◆ Make sauce

◆ Make dessert

SHOPPING LIST

PRODUCE
1 bag shredded ready-to-eat cabbage
1 bag shredded ready-to-eat carrots
1 small package fresh strawberries
1 red onion

DAIRY
1 can whipped cream topping, pressurized

SEAFOOD
3/4 lb large shrimp, peeled and deveined

GROCERY
1 bottle Key lime juice
1 small angel food cake

STAPLES
Reduced-fat mayonnaise
Dijon mustard
Ketchup
Hot pepper sauce
Sugar substitute
White vinegar
Salt
Black peppercorns

Nutrition Facts:
Key West Shrimp with
Key Lime Cocktail Sauce

Exchanges/Choices
1 Carbohydrate
3 Lean Meat

Calories	170
Calories from Fat	15
Total Fat	1.5 g
Saturated Fat	<1 g
Cholesterol	240 mg
Sodium	815 mg
Carbohydrate	13 g
Dietary Fiber	1 g
Sugars	5 g
Protein	27 g

Key West Shrimp

Preparation time: 5 minutes
Serves: 2/Serving size: 1/2 recipe

3/4 lb large shrimp, peeled and deveined
  1 Tbsp Key lime juice

1. Fill a medium saucepan three-quarters full with water. Add the shrimp and Key lime juice. Make sure the water covers the shrimp. Add more if needed.

2. Bring the water to a simmer with the bubbles just starting around the edge of the pot; the water will start to turn white. Take off the heat immediately and let sit 1 minute.

3. Drain the shrimp and plunge into cold water if serving cold or serve immediately if serving hot.

4. Serve with Key Lime Cocktail Sauce.

Key Lime Cocktail Sauce

6 Tbsp ketchup
   Several drops hot pepper sauce
2 tsp Key lime juice

1. Mix all ingredients together and taste.

2. Add seasoning if needed.

3. Serve with Key West Shrimp.

Nutrition Facts:
Quick Coleslaw

Exchanges/Choices
2 Vegetable
2 1/2 Fat

Calories	135
Calories from Fat	80
Total Fat	9 g
Saturated Fat	1.4 g
Cholesterol	5 mg
Sodium	275 mg
Carbohydrate	13 g
Dietary Fiber	3 g
Sugars	6 g
Protein	2 g

Quick Coleslaw

Preparation time: 5 minutes
Serves: 2/Serving size: 1/2 recipe

- 5 tsp reduced-fat mayonnaise
- 1/4 cup white vinegar
- 1 Tbsp Dijon mustard
  Sugar substitute equivalent to 1 tsp sugar
  Salt and fresh ground black pepper
- 2 cups shredded ready-to-eat cabbage
- 1/2 cup shredded ready-to-eat carrots
- 1/2 cup red onion, sliced

1. Mix mayonnaise, vinegar, mustard, sugar substitute, and salt and pepper to taste together in a medium-size bowl.

2. Add cabbage, carrot, and onion and toss well. Taste for seasoning and add more, if necessary.

Nutrition Facts:
Strawberries and Cream
Angel Food Cake

Exchanges/Choices
1 1/2 Carbohydrate

Calories	100
Calories from Fat	20
Total Fat	2 g
Saturated Fat	1 g
Cholesterol	5 mg
Sodium	120 mg
Carbohydrate	19 g
Dietary Fiber	2 g
Sugars	11 g
Protein	2 g

Strawberries and Cream Angel Food Cake

Preparation time: 5 minutes
Serves: 2/Serving size: 1/2 recipe

- 2 slices angel food cake (1 1/2 oz)
- 1 cup sliced strawberries
  Sugar substitute equivalent to 2 tsp sugar
- 1/4 cup whipped cream topping, pressurized

1. Place cake slices on two plates.

2. Mix strawberries and sugar substitute together and spoon over cake.

3. Top with whipped cream topping.

Speed Meals

These speed meals are based on ingredients you can quickly pick up in the supermarket and assemble in 15 minutes or less.

Poultry

Seafood

Pork

Veal

Beef

Paul Prudhomme's Bronzed Chicken Breasts

with Rice and Spinach Pilaf

Paul Prudhomme, considered the father of blackened redfish, gave me this tip: "My advice to people at home is bronzing rather that blackening. This avoids the smoke and the risk of handling a red-hot skillet while still achieving an excellent result." The coat of this bronzed chicken breast is golden and caramelized from the cooking method.

The secret to bronzing is keeping the skillet at the right temperature. The chicken should take 6–7 minutes to cook. If it takes much longer, the skillet is not hot enough.

Helpful Hints

♦ Cajun spice mixes can be found in the spice section of the supermarket.

♦ Boneless skinless chicken breast cutlets, about 1/2-inch thick, can be found in the meat section of the supermarket. Regular boneless skinless chicken breasts can be used instead. Pound these chicken breasts flat to about 1/2 to 3/4-inch thick with a meat bat or heavy skillet.

♦ An electric frying pan can be used instead of a skillet. Keep the temperature at 350°F.

Countdown

♦ Start rice and set aside

♦ Make chicken

♦ Finish rice

SHOPPING LIST

MEAT
3/4 lb boneless skinless chicken breast cutlets

GROCERY
1 small package Cajun or blackened spice seasoning mix
1 small jar/can no-salt-added tomato juice
1 package 10-minute brown rice

PRODUCE
1 10-oz package washed ready-to-eat spinach

STAPLES

Flour
Canola oil
Salt
Black peppercorns

Bronzed Chicken Breasts

Preparation time: 8 minutes
Serves 2/Serving size: 1/2 recipe

- 2 Tbsp Cajun or blackened spice seasoning mix
- 1 Tbsp flour
- 3/4 lb boneless skinless chicken breast cutlets
- 2 tsp canola oil

1. Mix Cajun seasoning and flour together.

2. Spoon 1 tablespoon of the spice mixture onto one side of the chicken breast cutlets, pressing it into the flesh.

3. Heat a medium-sized nonstick skillet over high heat and add oil. When it is very hot, add the chicken breasts, seasoned side down. Spread remaining spice mixture on top side of chicken.

4. Cook until the underside is bronze in color, about 2–3 minutes. Cook second side 3–4 minutes or until cooked through. A meat thermometer should read 170°F.

Nutrition Facts:
Bronzed Chicken Breasts

Exchanges/Choices
1/2 Carbohydrate
5 Lean Meat

Calories	260
Calories from Fat	80
Total Fat	9 g
Saturated Fat	1.5 g
Cholesterol	100 mg
Sodium	615 mg
Carbohydrate	5 g
Dietary Fiber	0 g
Sugars	0 g
Protein	37 g

Rice and Spinach Pilaf

Preparation time: 10 minutes
Serves 2/Serving size: 1/2 recipe

- 1/2 cup water
- 1/2 cup no-added-salt tomato juice
- 1/2 cup 10-minute brown rice
- 2 cups washed ready-to-eat spinach
- 1 tsp canola oil
  Salt and freshly ground black pepper

1. Bring water and tomato juice to a boil in a medium-size saucepan over high heat.

2. Add the rice, cover, and simmer 5 minutes.

3. Remove from heat, add the spinach, replace the cover, and let sit 5 minutes.

4. Add oil and salt and pepper to taste.

5. Toss well.

Nutrition Facts:
Rice and Spinach Pilaf

Exchanges/Choices
2 1/2 Starch
1 Vegetable

Calories	209
Calories from Fat	34
Total Fat	4 g
Saturated Fat	<1 g
Cholesterol	0 mg
Sodium	33 mg
Carbohydrate	39 g
Dietary Fiber	3 g
Sugars	5 g
Protein	5 g

Buffalo Chicken
with Hot Pepper Brown Rice

Here's a new take on the classic blue cheese and buffalo sauce combination. The tangy cheese flavor complements the spiciness of the hot pepper sauce, creating a quick and tasty new addition to your game-day menu.

Helpful Hints

♦ Any type of cooked chicken breast with bones and skin removed can be used instead of cooked chicken strips.

♦ Blue cheese already crumbled can be found in the dairy section of the supermarket.

Countdown

♦ Start rice

♦ While rice cooks, make chicken

SHOPPING LIST

DAIRY
1 small package crumbled blue cheese

MEAT
3/4 lb cooked chicken breast strips

GROCERY
1 small can/bottle no-salt-added
tomato sauce

PRODUCE
1 package 10-minute brown rice

STAPLES
Celery
Fat-free milk
Hot pepper sauce
Canola oil

Buffalo Chicken

Preparation time: 5 minutes
Serves 2/Serving size: 1/2 recipe

1/2	cup fat-free milk
1 1/2	Tbsp crumbled blue cheese (3/4 oz)
3/4	lb cooked chicken breast strips

1. Warm milk in a medium-size skillet over medium-high heat. Add cheese and stir to melt.

2. When the cheese starts to melt, add chicken to warm through.

3. Simmer 3–4 minutes to reduce sauce. Add pepper to taste. The cheese should provide the salt.

	245
Calories from Fat	45
Total Fat	5 g
Saturated Fat	2 g
Cholesterol	100 mg
Sodium	690 mg
Carbohydrate	4 g
Dietary Fiber	0 g
Sugars	3 g
Protein	43 g

Hot Pepper Brown Rice

Preparation time: 11 minutes
Serves 2/Serving size: 1/2 recipe

1/2	cup no-salt-added tomato sauce
1/2	cup water
1	cup sliced celery
1/2	cup 10-minute brown rice
	Several drops hot pepper sauce
1	tsp canola oil

1. Add tomato sauce, water, celery, and rice to a medium-size saucepan.

2. Bring to a boil over high heat, lower heat to medium-low, cover with a lid, and simmer 10 minutes. If rice becomes dry, add a little more water.

3. Add hot pepper sauce and canola oil. Toss well.

Nutrition Facts:
Hot Pepper Brown Rice

Exchanges/Choices
2 1/2 Starch
1 Vegetable

Calories	216
Calories from Fat	33
Total Fat	3 g
Saturated Fat	<1 g
Cholesterol	0 mg
Sodium	67 mg
Carbohydrate	41 g
Dietary Fiber	3 g
Sugars	5 g
Protein	5 g

Chicken Chili

with Brown Rice and Salad

Forget the slow cooker and the all-day kitchen duty. You can prepare this satisfying chili in no time. Served with salad, it is a tantalizing combination of spicy and refreshing flavors.

Helpful Hints

◆ Microwaveable brown rice is sold in most supermarkets and cooks in 90 seconds. If not available, use 10-minute brown rice.

◆ Two medium garlic cloves or crushed garlic can be used instead of minced garlic in a jar.

Countdown

◆ Start chili

◆ Make rice

◆ Assemble salad

SHOPPING LIST

MEAT
1/2 lb cooked boneless skinless chicken strips

GROCERY
2 cans chopped tomatoes
1 can red kidney beans
1 package chili seasoning mix
1 package microwave brown rice
1 package frozen chopped onion

PRODUCE
1 package washed ready-to-eat salad
1 bottle minced garlic

STAPLES
Canola oil
Reduced-fat oil and vinegar salad dressing

Nutrition Facts:
Chicken Chili

Exchanges/Choices
3 1/2 Starch
4 Vegetable
3 Lean Meat

Calories	530
Calories from Fat	80
Total Fat	9 g
Saturated Fat	<1 g
Cholesterol	60 mg
Sodium	1,310 mg
Carbohydrate	74 g
Dietary Fiber	13 g
Sugars	14 g
Protein	41 g

Chicken Chili

Preparation time: 10 minutes
Serves 2/Serving size: 1/2 recipe

2 tsp canola oil
1 cup frozen chopped onion
2 tsp minced garlic
2 cups canned chopped tomatoes
3/4 cup rinsed and drained canned red kidney beans
3 Tbsp chili seasoning mix
1/2 lb boneless skinless cooked chicken strips
1 cup microwave brown rice

1. Heat oil in a medium-size saucepan over medium-high heat.

2. Add the onion and garlic and sauté 1 minute.

3. Add the chopped tomatoes, kidney beans, and chili seasoning.

4. Simmer 5 minutes. Reduce heat to low and add chicken.

5. Cook 2–3 minutes or until chicken is warmed through.

6. Meanwhile, make rice according to package instructions. Measure 3/4 cup cooked rice per person.

Nutrition Facts:
Salad

Exchanges/Choices
1/2 Fat

Calories	35
Calories from Fat	20
Total Fat	2.5 g
Saturated Fat	<1 g
Cholesterol	0 mg
Sodium	150 mg
Carbohydrate	3 g
Dietary Fiber	1 g
Sugars	2 g
Protein	1 g

Salad

Preparation time: 2 minutes
Serves 2/Serving size: 1/2 recipe

2 cups washed ready-to-eat salad
2 Tbsp reduced-fat oil and vinegar salad dressing

1. Place salad in a bowl and mix in dressing.

Chicken Fajitas

with Hot Pepper Tomatoes

Fajitas, warm tortillas filled with savory chicken and crunchy vegetables, are a meal in a wrap.

Helpful Hints

♦ Look for prepackaged boneless skinless chicken breast cut for stir-fry. Or use boneless skinless chicken breast and cut into strips.

♦ To save prep time, buy sliced onion and red pepper at a salad bar. Or, slice them using the slicing blade of a food processor.

♦ Green or yellow bell peppers can be used.

♦ For the fajita sauce, look for approximately 300 g sodium and 5 g carbohydrates per tablespoon.

Countdown

♦ Assemble ingredients

♦ Prepare fajitas

SHOPPING LIST

DAIRY
1 small carton reduced-fat
    sour cream

MEAT
3/4 lb boneless skinless
    chicken breast cut for stir-fry

GROCERY
1 small bottle fajita sauce
1 small package 8-inch
    whole-wheat tortillas

PRODUCE
1 red bell pepper
2 medium tomatoes

STAPLES

Onion
Canola oil
Salt
Black peppercorns
Hot pepper sauce

Nutrition Facts:
Chicken Fajitas

Exchanges/Choices
2 1/2 Starch
1/2 Carbohydrate
1 Vegetable
5 Lean Meat
1 Fat

Calories	555
Calories from Fat	115
Total Fat	13 g
Saturated Fat	1.8 g
Cholesterol	95 mg
Sodium	1,370 mg
Carbohydrate	58 g
Dietary Fiber	8 g
Sugars	15 g
Protein	48 g

Chicken Fajitas

Preparation time: 5 minutes
Serves: 2/Serving size: 1/2 recipe

     2 tsp canola oil
   1/2 cup sliced onion
     1 cup sliced red bell pepper
   3/4 lb prepackaged boneless skinless chicken breast cut for stir-fry
   1/4 cup bottled fajita sauce
        Salt and freshly ground black pepper
     4 8-inch whole-wheat tortillas
     2 Tbsp reduced-fat sour cream

1. Heat oil in a medium-size nonstick skillet over high heat.

2. Add the onion, bell pepper, and chicken. Cook 2 minutes.

3. Add the fajita sauce and continue to cook 2 minutes. Add salt and pepper to taste.

4. Place tortillas on paper towels in a microwave oven for 15 seconds or wrap in foil and place in a toaster oven at 350°F for 5 minutes. Remove and place one each on two plates. Keep other two wrapped to stay warm.

5. To serve, spoon some of the chicken and vegetables onto each of the tortillas and add 1/2 tablespoon sour cream to each one. Wrap and serve.

Nutrition Facts:
Hot Pepper Tomatoes

Exchanges/Choices
1 Vegetable

Calories	20
Calories from Fat	0
Total Fat	0 g
Saturated Fat	<1 g
Cholesterol	0 mg
Sodium	5 mg
Carbohydrate	5 g
Dietary Fiber	1 g
Sugars	3 g
Protein	1 g

Hot Pepper Tomatoes

Preparation time: 1 minute
Serves 2/Serving size: 1/2 recipe

     2 medium tomatoes, sliced
        Hot pepper sauce (optional)

1. Place tomatoes on a plate and sprinkle hot sauce on top.

Chicken Pita Pocket with Tomato and Corn Salsa

with Greek Salad

Roasted chicken garnished with refreshing tomato and corn salsa is stuffed in a pita bread to make this quick supper. Let the supermarket do the work. Make the fresh salsa using diced tomatoes found in the produce section or at the salad bar and add some defrosted frozen corn.

For the Greek Salad side dish, doctor up washed ready-to-eat salad with sliced bell peppers and cucumber from the salad bar. Add oregano to a bottled salad dressing for a Greek flavor and toss olives into the salad.

Helpful Hints

◆ If diced tomatoes are not available, use a bottled chunky salsa instead of making the one in the recipe.

◆ Boneless skinless chicken breast strips can be used instead of roasted chicken breast.

Countdown

◆ Prepare tomato and corn salsa and set aside to marinate a few minutes

◆ Make the Greek Salad

◆ Complete the pita pockets

SHOPPING LIST

DAIRY
1 small package reduced-fat crumbled feta cheese

MEAT
3/4 lb boneless roasted or rotisserie chicken breast

GROCERY
1 package whole-wheat pita breads (6 1/2 inches in diameter each)
1 package frozen corn kernels

PRODUCE
1 container diced tomatoes
1 lime
1 bag washed ready-to-eat lettuce
1 small bunch cilantro (optional)

STAPLES

Ground cumin
Olive oil
Hot pepper sauce
Reduced-fat oil and vinegar salad dressing
Salt
Black peppercorns

Nutrition Facts:
Chicken Pita Pocket with Tomato and Corn Salsa

Exchanges/Choices
3 Starch
6 Lean Meat

Calories	525
Calories from Fat	110
Total Fat	12 g
Saturated Fat	2.5 g
Cholesterol	130 mg
Sodium	465 mg
Carbohydrate	48 g
Dietary Fiber	7 g
Sugars	4 g
Protein	57 g

Chicken Pita Pocket with Tomato and Corn Salsa

Preparation time: 5 minutes
Serves 2/Serving size: 1/2 recipe

1/2	cup frozen corn kernels
1	cup diced tomatoes (buy ready diced)
	Several drops hot pepper sauce
1 1/2	tsp ground cumin
	Salt and freshly ground black pepper
1	Tbsp lime juice
2	tsp olive oil
2	whole-wheat pita breads (6 1/2 inches in diameter each)
3/4	lb boneless roasted or rotisserie chicken breast, skin removed, cut into strips
3	Tbsp chopped fresh cilantro (optional)

1. Place corn in a microwave-safe bowl and microwave on high for 2 minutes to defrost. Mix tomatoes and hot pepper sauce with the corn.

2. Add the cumin and salt and pepper to taste. Add lime juice and oil and toss well.

3. Toast pita bread in a toaster oven to warm slightly. Do not let it get too crisp. Cut pita breads in half and open pockets.

4. Spoon half the salsa into the pockets. Add the chicken and finish with the remaining salsa. Top with cilantro and serve.

Nutrition Facts:
Greek Salad

Exchanges/Choices
1 Fat

Calories	50
Calories from Fat	35
Total Fat	4 g
Saturated Fat	1.3 g
Cholesterol	5 g
Sodium	225 mg
Carbohydrate	2 g
Dietary Fiber	1 g
Sugars	2 g
Protein	2 g

Greek Salad

Preparation time: 2 minutes
Serves 2/Serving size: 1/2 recipe

2	cups washed ready-to-eat lettuce
2	Tbsp reduced-fat crumbled feta cheese
2	Tbsp light vinaigrette dressing

1. Place the lettuce and feta cheese in a bowl.

2. Add dressing and toss well.

Cajun Kabobs

with Creole Rice and Red Beans

These kabobs offer Cajun taste in just a flash. Just dip chicken cubes in the spice mixture and broil for 5 minutes.

Helpful Hints

◆ Canned small red kidney beans can be found in most markets. The smaller size gives a better texture to the dish, but regular red beans can be used.

◆ Warm the beans and chicken stock in a microwave oven to save cooking and cleanup time.

Countdown

◆ Preheat broiler

◆ Start rice

◆ Make kabobs

SHOPPING LIST

MEAT
3/4 lb boneless skinless
  chicken breast

GROCERY
1 box 10-minute brown rice
1 can small red Kidney beans
1 package Cajun or blackened
  spice seasoning

PRODUCE
6 oz zucchini
6 oz yellow squash

STAPLES
Hot pepper sauce
Olive oil spray
Olive oil
Salt
Black peppercorns

Nutrition Facts:
Cajun Kabobs

Exchanges/Choices
1 Vegetable
5 Lean Meat

Calories	250
Calories from Fat	65
Total Fat	7 g
Saturated Fat	1.5 g
Cholesterol	100 mg
Sodium	395 mg
Carbohydrate	8 g
Dietary Fiber	2 g
Sugars	3 g
Protein	39 g

Cajun Kabobs

Preparation time: 6 minutes
Serves 2/Serving size: 1/2 recipe

	Olive oil spray
3/4	Tbsp Cajun or blackened spice seasoning
3/4	lb boneless skinless chicken breast, cut into 1-inch pieces
1	tsp olive oil
	Salt and freshly ground pepper
6	oz zucchini (about 1 cup)
6	oz yellow squash (about 1 cup)

1. Preheat broiler.
2. Line a baking tray with foil and spray with olive oil spray. Place on rack about 5 inches from heat.
3. Place Cajun spice seasoning in a bowl.
4. Spray chicken cubes with olive oil spray. Toss in the spice mixture. Divide cubes in half and thread on two skewers.
5. Place olive oil in a small bowl and add salt and pepper to taste.
6. Cut zucchini and yellow squash into 1-inch pieces and toss in oil to coat.
7. Divide in half and place on two skewers, alternating the vegetables.
8. Remove tray from oven and place the skewers on the foil.
9. Return to oven and broil 3 minutes. Turn skewers over and broil 2 minutes.

Nutrition Facts:
Creole Rice and
Red Beans

Exchanges/Choices
3 1/2 Starch
1/2 Fat

Calories	300
Calories from Fat	35
Total Fat	4 g
Saturated Fat	<1 g
Cholesterol	0 mg
Sodium	170 mg
Carbohydrate	56 g
Dietary Fiber	7 g
Sugars	2 g
Protein	11 g

Creole Rice and Red Beans

Preparation time: 10 minutes
Serves 2/Serving size: 1/2 recipe

1/2	cup 10-minute brown rice
1	cup water
1	cup canned small red kidney beans, rinsed and drained
	Several drops hot pepper sauce
1	tsp olive oil
	Salt and freshly ground black pepper to taste

1. Add rice and water to a medium-size saucepan.
2. Bring to a boil over high heat, lower heat to medium, and simmer 10 minutes.
3. Stir in kidney beans, hot pepper sauce, and olive oil. Add salt and pepper to taste. Mix well.

Three-Bean Chicken Toss

The oil and vinegar dressing brightens up the flavors of the chicken and beans. The whole-wheat baguette with Parmesan cheese complements this delicious and unconventional chicken and bean salad.

Helpful Hints

♦ Buy trimmed green beans and cut them into 1-inch pieces.

♦ Toast baguette with cheese in a toaster oven or under a broiler.

♦ Use same bowl for microwaving green beans and making the salad.

Countdown

♦ Toast baguette

♦ Make salad

SHOPPING LIST

MEAT
3/4 lb cooked boneless
    skinless chicken strips

GROCERY
1 whole-wheat baguette
1 small can chickpeas
1 small can red Kidney beans

PRODUCE
1/4 lb trimmed green beans

STAPLES

Parmesan cheese
Reduced-fat oil and vinegar
    salad dressing
Salt
Black peppercorns

Nutrition Facts:
Three-Bean Chicken Toss

Exchanges/Choices
4 Starch
6 Lean Meat

Calories	585
Calories from Fat	110
Total Fat	12 g
Saturated Fat	2.1 g
Cholesterol	95 mg
Sodium	1,320 mg
Carbohydrate	64 g
Dietary Fiber	11 g
Sugars	8 g
Protein	58 g

Three-Bean Chicken Toss

Preparation time: 5 minutes
Serves 2/Serving size: 1/2 recipe

1/2 whole-wheat baguette (6 inches)
  2 Tbsp grated Parmesan cheese
1/4 lb trimmed green beans, cut into 1-inch lengths (about 1 cup)
3/4 lb cooked boneless skinless chicken strips
1/2 cup drained and rinsed chickpeas
1/2 cup drained and rinsed red kidney beans
1/4 cup reduced-fat oil and vinegar salad dressing
    Salt and freshly ground black pepper

1. Slice baguette in half lengthwise and then in half horizontally to make two pieces.

2. Sprinkle with Parmesan cheese and place in toaster oven to melt cheese, about 2 minutes.

3. Place green beans in a large microwave-safe bowl and microwave on high 2 minutes.

4. Remove from microwave and add chicken, chickpeas, kidney beans, and dressing. Toss well.

5. Add salt and pepper to taste. Toss again.

6. Serve with Parmesan baguette.

Honey Pepper Turkey
with Pimento Pasta

Turkey is not just for Thanksgiving anymore. The sweet and savory flavors of the sauce are a delicious and unexpected variation on traditional turkey cutlets. The smoky flavor of the pimento pasta complements the sauce.

Helpful Hints

♦ Thin-sliced, boneless skinless turkey breast is available in most markets. Thin-sliced boneless, skinless chicken breast can be used instead.

♦ Cracked black pepper can be found in the spice section of the supermarket.

♦ If using thicker sliced turkey or chicken, cook until a meat thermometer reaches 170°F.

Countdown

♦ Place water for pasta on to boil

♦ Make turkey

♦ Make Pimento Pasta

SHOPPING LIST

MEAT
3/4 lb turkey breast cutlets
    (1/4 to 1/2-inch thick)

GROCERY
1 small jar honey
1 jar/can sliced, roasted red peppers
1 bottle cracked pepper
1 package whole-wheat linguine

STAPLES
Worcestershire sauce
Dijon mustard
Canola oil
Salt
Black peppercorns

Nutrition Facts:
Honey Pepper Turkey

Exchanges/Choices
1 1/2 Carbohydrate
5 Lean Meat
1/2 Fat

Calories	350
Calories from Fat	90
Total Fat	10 g
Saturated Fat	1 g
Cholesterol	110 mg
Sodium	530 mg
Carbohydrate	22 g
Dietary Fiber	1 g
Sugars	20 g
Protein	41 g

Honey Pepper Turkey

Preparation time: 5 minutes
Serves 2/Serving size: 1/2 recipe

1	Tbsp Worcestershire sauce
2	Tbsp honey
2	Tbsp Dijon mustard
1/2	tsp cracked pepper
4	tsp canola oil
3/4	lb boneless skinless turkey breast cutlets (1/4 to 1/2-inch thick)

1. Mix Worcestershire sauce, honey, Dijon mustard, and cracked pepper together and set aside.

2. Heat oil in a medium-size nonstick skillet over medium-high heat.

3. Add turkey and brown 1 minute. Turn and brown second side 1 minute. Reduce heat to low, spoon sauce over turkey and cook 1 minute.

Nutrition Facts:
Pimento Pasta

Exchanges/Choices
3 Starch
1 Fat

Calories	260
Calories from Fat	55
Total Fat	6 g
Saturated Fat	<1 g
Cholesterol	0 mg
Sodium	85 mg
Carbohydrate	44 g
Dietary Fiber	4 g
Sugars	4 g
Protein	8 g

Pimento Pasta

Preparation time: 9 minutes
Serves 2/Serving size: 1/2 recipe

1/4	lb whole-wheat linguine
1/2	cup drained, canned, sliced roasted red peppers
2	tsp canola oil
	Salt and freshly ground black pepper

1. Fill a large saucepan with water and bring to a boil.

2. Add the linguine and cook 8 minutes or until pasta is al dente. Drain.

3. Add the roasted red peppers, canola oil, and salt and pepper to taste.

Dijon Scallops
with Carrots and Rice

This simple and elegant dish is sure to impress your family and guests. The creamy Dijon sauce is accented with the light onion taste of the chives. The addition of carrots to the rice adds a sweet new dimension to the side dish.

Helpful Hints

◆ Buy frozen scallops and keep in freezer for quick meals. They will defrost under cold water in about 5 minutes.

◆ Freeze-dried chives can be substituted.

◆ A quick way to chop chives is to snip them with scissors.

Countdown

◆ Start rice

◆ Make scallops

◆ Assemble dinner

SHOPPING LIST

DAIRY
1 small carton heavy cream

SEAFOOD
3/4 lb scallops

GROCERY
1 small bottle sherry
1 box 10-minute brown rice

PRODUCE
1 small bunch chives
1 package grated or shredded carrots

STAPLES
Canola oil
Dijon mustard
Salt
Black peppercorns

Dijon Scallops

Preparation time: 4 minutes
Serves 2/Serving size: 1/2 recipe

2	tsp canola oil
3/4	lb scallops
1/2	cup dry sherry
2	Tbsp Dijon mustard
1	Tbsp heavy cream
2	Tbsp chopped chives
	Salt and freshly ground black pepper

1. Heat oil in a medium-size nonstick skillet. Add scallops to pan and sauté 1 minute per side. Remove scallops to a dish. Add sherry to pan and simmer 30 seconds. Add mustard and cream to pan and mix well.

2. Return scallops to pan for 30 seconds. Add salt and pepper to taste. Sprinkle chives on top.

3. Serve scallops over rice and carrots.

Nutrition Facts:
Dijon Scallops

Exchanges/Choices
1/2 Carbohydrate
4 Lean Meat
1 Fat

Calories	290
Calories from Fat	90
Total Fat	10 g
Saturated Fat	2.3 g
Cholesterol	80 mg
Sodium	705 mg
Carbohydrate	8 g
Dietary Fiber	1 g
Sugars	1 g
Protein	31 g

Carrots and Rice

Preparation time: 10 minutes
Serves 2/Serving size: 1/2 recipe

1/2	cup 10-minute brown rice
1	cup water
1/2	cup packaged grated carrots
	Salt and freshly ground black pepper

1. Add rice and water to a medium-size saucepan and bring to a boil.

2. Lower heat to medium, add carrots, cover with a lid, and simmer 10 minutes. Add salt and pepper to taste.

3. Divide between two plates and serve scallops and sauce on top.

Nutrition Facts:
Carrots and Rice

Exchanges/Choices
2 1/2 Starch

Calories	175
Calories from Fat	15
Total Fat	1.5 g
Saturated Fat	0 g
Cholesterol	0 mg
Sodium	40 mg
Carbohydrate	39 g
Dietary Fiber	2 g
Sugars	2 g
Protein	4 g

Roasted Pepper and Olive Snapper

with Green Pepper Rice

Fresh snapper, roasted red peppers, and Greek olives broiled for only 8 minutes make a simple Mediterranean meal.

Helpful Hints

♦ Any type of olive can be used.

♦ Any type of fish fillet can be used. Count 10 minutes cooking time for each inch of thickness.

Countdown

♦ Preheat broiler

♦ Start rice

♦ Make snapper

♦ Finish rice

SHOPPING LIST

SEAFOOD
2 6-oz snapper fillets

GROCERY
2 cans/jars sliced roasted
   red peppers
1 container pitted black olives
1 box 10-minute brown rice
1 package diced or chopped
   frozen green pepper

STAPLES

Olive oil
Fat-free, reduced-sodium
   chicken broth
Salt
Black peppercorns

Roasted Pepper and Olive Snapper

Nutrition Facts:
Roasted Pepper and
Olive Snapper

Exchanges/Choices
2 Vegetable
5 Lean Meat
1/2 Fat

Calories	305
Calories from Fat	100
Total Fat	**11 g**
Saturated Fat	1.6 g
Cholesterol	**60 mg**
Sodium	**605 mg**
Carbohydrate	**13 g**
Dietary Fiber	2 g
Sugars	6 g
Protein	**37 g**

Preparation time: 10 minutes
Serves 2/Serving size: 1/2 recipe

 2 6-oz snapper fillets
 1 Tbsp olive oil
   Salt and freshly ground black pepper
 1 1/2 cups canned/jarred sliced roasted red peppers
 8 pitted black olives, cut in half

1. Preheat broiler. Wash fillet and pat dry with paper towel.

2. Place in small, shallow ovenproof dish. Drizzle olive oil on top. Sprinkle with salt and pepper to taste.

3. Place roasted pepper slices over fish. Cut olives in half and place on peppers. Broil 8 minutes. If fillet is 1-inch thick, broil 10 minutes.

Green Pepper Rice

Nutrition Facts:
Green Pepper Rice

Exchanges/Choices
2 1/2 Starch

Calories	200
Calories from Fat	30
Total Fat	**3.5 g**
Saturated Fat	<1 g
Cholesterol	**0 mg**
Sodium	**270 mg**
Carbohydrate	**39 g**
Dietary Fiber	2 g
Sugars	2 g
Protein	**5 g**

Preparation time: 12 minutes
Serves 2/Serving size: 1/2 recipe

 1/2 cup 10-minute brown rice
  1 cup fat-free reduced-sodium chicken broth
 1/2 cup diced or chopped frozen green pepper
  1 tsp olive oil
    Salt and freshly ground black pepper

1. Add rice and chicken broth to a medium-size saucepan and bring to a boil.

2. Add green pepper, cover with a lid, lower heat to medium, and simmer 10 minutes. Rice will be cooked and liquid evaporated. If rice becomes too dry before it is finished cooking, add a little more broth.

3. Add olive oil and salt and pepper to taste.

Almond-Crusted Trout

with Penne and Sugar Snap Peas

Fresh trout topped with almond crumbs takes only minutes to make. Farm-raised trout is available in many markets, usually with the bones removed and sometimes without the head and tail. If you prefer, ask for the head and tail to be removed. Toasting almonds intensifies their flavor. This can be done in a toaster oven or under a broiler.

If trout is not available, use any type of fish fillet (tilapia, grouper, mahi-mahi, flounder, or sole). Measure the fish at its thickest part and cook for 10 minutes per inch of thickness.

Helpful Hints

◆ Buy frozen trout to keep on hand for quick meals.

◆ Buy trimmed sugar snap peas.

◆ Green beans or snow peas can be used instead of sugar snap peas.

◆ Any short cut pasta can be used.

◆ Curly parsley can be used instead of flat parsley.

Countdown

◆ Place water for pasta on to boil

◆ Prepare ingredients

◆ Toast the almonds

◆ Cook the pasta

◆ While pasta cooks, sauté the trout

SHOPPING LIST

SEAFOOD
2 whole trout, about 6 oz each, with heads, tails, and bones removed

GROCERY
1 small package whole almonds
1/4 lb whole-wheat penne pasta

PRODUCE
1/2 lb trimmed sugar snap peas
1 small bunch flat-leaf parsley (optional)

STAPLES
Olive oil spray
Reduced-fat oil and vinegar salad dressing
Salt
Black peppercorns

Almond-Crusted Trout

Preparation time: 12 minutes
Serves 2/Serving size: 1/2 recipe

Nutrition Facts:
Almond-Crusted Trout

Exchanges/Choices
5 Lean Meat
2 1/2 Fat

Calories	355
Calories from Fat	180
Total Fat	20 g
Saturated Fat	2.7 g
Cholesterol	100 mg
Sodium	90 mg
Carbohydrate	3 g
Dietary Fiber	2 g
Sugars	1 g
Protein	39 g

1/4 cup whole almonds
2 trout (about 6 oz each) with heads, tail, and bones removed
   Salt and freshly ground black pepper
   Olive oil spray
2 Tbsp chopped flat-leaf parsley (optional)

1. Coarsely grind almonds in a food processor or blender, or finely chop by hand.

2. Heat a nonstick skillet over medium-high heat. Add ground almonds and toast 1 minute or until golden. Open trout flat. Season with salt and pepper to taste.

3. Place the same skillet over high heat. Spray with olive oil spray and add trout. Sauté 5 minutes, then turn and sauté an additional 4 minutes.

4. Remove and place on two dinner plates and scatter almond crust over trout. Sprinkle parsley on top.

Penne with Sugar Snap Peas

Preparation time: 12 minutes
Serves 2/Serving size: 1/2 recipe

Nutrition Facts:
Penne with
Sugar Snap Peas

Exchanges/Choices
3 Starch
1/2 Fat

Calories	250
Calories from Fat	30
Total Fat	3.5 g
Saturated Fat	<1 g
Cholesterol	0 mg
Sodium	150 mg
Carbohydrate	48 g
Dietary Fiber	7 g
Sugars	5 g
Protein	8 g

1/4 lb whole-wheat penne pasta
1/2 lb sugar snap peas, trimmed
2 Tbsp reduced-fat oil and vinegar salad dressing
   Salt and freshly ground black pepper

1. Bring a large saucepan with 3–4 quarts of water to a boil. Add penne pasta and boil 7 minutes.

2. Add the sugar snap peas and continue to boil 2–3 minutes or until pasta is cooked al dente.

3. Drain, leaving about 1 Tbsp cooking water on the pasta. Toss with salad dressing and salt and pepper to taste.

Wild Salmon

with Asparagus and Roasted Pepper Penne Pasta

Wild salmon is so flavorful, it only needs a little olive oil and salt and pepper and it cooks in minutes. It's available fresh from mid-May until mid-September. At other times of the year, good quality wild salmon can be found in the frozen seafood section of the supermarket. King salmon (also called Chinook), coho, and sockeye are some of the wild salmon varieties to look for.

Helpful Hints

♦ If you can't find wild salmon, farmed salmon can be used for this recipe. The flavor will be different.

♦ A quick way to chop dill is to wash, dry, and snip the leaves right off the stem. Dried dill can be used.

Countdown

♦ Preheat oven

♦ Boil water for pasta

♦ Prepare and bake salmon

♦ Finish pasta dish

SHOPPING LIST

SEAFOOD
3/4 lb fresh wild salmon with skin

GROCERY
1/4 lb whole-wheat penne pasta
1 bottle/can sliced roasted
    red pepper

PRODUCE
1 lb fresh asparagus
1 small bunch dill

STAPLES

Olive oil spray
Olive oil
Salt
Black peppercorns

Nutrition Facts:
Wild Salmon

Exchanges/Choices
6 Lean Meat

Calories	250
Calories from Fat	70
Total Fat	**8 g**
Saturated Fat	1.9 g
Cholesterol	**100 mg**
Sodium	**105 mg**
Carbohydrate	**0 g**
Dietary Fiber	0 g
Sugars	0 g
Protein	**42 g**

Wild Salmon

Preparation time: 12 minutes
Serves 2/Serving size: 1/2 recipe

> Olive oil spray
> 3/4 lb fresh wild salmon with skin
> Salt and freshly ground black pepper to taste
> 1 tsp snipped dill

1. Preheat oven to 425°F. Line a baking tray with foil and spray with olive oil spray. Place salmon, skin side down, on tray.

2. Spray salmon with olive oil spray and sprinkle with salt and pepper to taste. Place on middle shelf in oven for 10 minutes or until salmon is just cooked through. When a knife is inserted, the flesh should be opaque not translucent. Do not overcook. The salmon will continue to cook in its own heat when removed from the oven.

3. Sprinkle the salmon with the dill and serve.

Nutrition Facts:
Asparagus and Roasted Pepper Penne Pasta

Exchanges/Choices
3 Starch
1/2 Fat

Calories	260
Calories from Fat	30
Total Fat	**3.5 g**
Saturated Fat	0.5 g
Cholesterol	**0 mg**
Sodium	**85 mg**
Carbohydrate	**50 g**
Dietary Fiber	10 g
Sugars	7 g
Protein	**11 g**

Asparagus and Roasted Pepper Penne Pasta

Preparation time: 12 minutes
Serves 2/Serving size: 1/2 recipe

> 1/4 lb whole-wheat penne pasta
> 1 lb fresh asparagus, cut into 2-inch pieces (about 2 cups)
> 2 tsp olive oil
> 1/2 cup bottled/canned sliced roasted red pepper, drained
> Salt and freshly ground black pepper to taste

1. Bring a large saucepan with 3–4 quarts of water to a boil.

2. Add the penne pasta and boil 5 minutes. Add the asparagus and continue to boil 3 to 4 minutes or until pasta is cooked al dente.

3. Drain, leaving about 2 Tbsp of the boiling water in the pan.

4. Add olive oil to the water in the pan and return the pasta to the pan. Toss well. Add the red pepper and salt and pepper to taste.

Pork Pizzaioli

with Fennel and White Bean Salad

Have a meal your Italian nonna *would be proud of. The simple yet satisfying combination of tomato, olive, and garlic on the pork pairs beautifully with the earthiness of the beans and the surprising bite of fennel bulb in the salad.*

Helpful Hints

◆ One medium garlic clove, crushed, can be used instead of minced garlic.

◆ Cannellini beans can be used instead of navy beans.

◆ Slice fennel in a food processor fitted with a slicing blade.

◆ Sliced celery can be used instead of fennel.

Countdown

◆ Make salad and let marinate in dressing while pork cooks

◆ Make pork

SHOPPING LIST

MEAT
3/4 lb pork tenderloin

GROCERY
1 small jar/can low-sodium pasta sauce
1 jar/can pitted black olives
1 small can white navy beans
1 bottle low-fat Italian dressing

PRODUCE
1 fennel bulb
1 bottle minced garlic

STAPLES
Hot pepper sauce
Olive oil spray
Salt
Black peppercorns

Nutrition Facts:
Pork Pizzaioli

Exchanges/Choices
1/2 Starch
5 Lean Meat

Calories	255
Calories from Fat	65
Total Fat	7 g
Saturated Fat	2 g
Cholesterol	90 mg
Sodium	450 mg
Carbohydrate	10 g
Dietary Fiber	1 g
Sugars	6 g
Protein	34 g

Pork Pizzaioli

Preparation time: 15 minutes
Serves 2/Serving size: 1/2 recipe

- 1/2 cup low-sodium pasta sauce
- 4 pitted black olives, cut in half
  Several drops hot pepper sauce
  Salt and freshly ground black pepper
- 3/4 lb pork tenderloin
- 2 tsp minced garlic
  Olive oil spray

1. Place pasta sauce and olives in a microwave-safe bowl.

2. Cover and microwave on high 2 minutes, or place in a medium-size saucepan and simmer 2 minutes or until heated through.

3. Add the hot pepper sauce and salt and pepper to taste to the warmed sauce. Cover and remove from heat while pork cooks.

4. Cut the pork almost in half, lengthwise. Do not cut all the way through. It should open like a book.

5. Heat a medium-size nonstick skillet over medium-high heat and spray with olive oil spray. Add the garlic and pork. Brown the pork 2 minutes. Turn over and brown second side 2 minutes. Salt and pepper the cooked side.

6. Lower heat to medium, cover with a lid, and cook for 4 additional minutes. A meat thermometer should read 160°F.

7. Remove from the skillet, cut in half, and spoon sauce on top.

Nutrition Facts:
Fennel and White
Bean Salad

Exchanges/Choices
2 Starch
1 Vegetable
1/2 Fat

Calories	195
Calories from Fat	20
Total Fat	2.5 g
Saturated Fat	<1 g
Cholesterol	0 mg
Sodium	625 mg
Carbohydrate	37 g
Dietary Fiber	10 g
Sugars	8 g
Protein	10 g

Fennel and White Bean Salad

Preparation time: 3 minutes
Serves 2/Serving size: 1/2 recipe

> 1 large fennel bulb, thinly sliced (about 3 cups)
> 1 cup drained and rinsed white navy beans
> 3 Tbsp low-fat Italian salad dressing
> Salt and freshly ground black pepper

1. Cut the top stem and feathery leaves off the fennel. Reserve the fennel leaves. Wash and slice the fennel bulb.

2. Place sliced fennel and beans in a bowl and add dressing and salt and pepper to taste. Toss well. Snip about 1 tablespoon of the feathery leaves and sprinkle over salad.

Pork and Apple Butter Sauce

with Quick Barley and Lima Beans

Savory and sweet apple butter sauce flavors succulent pork chops, while quick-cooking barley and green beans make a crunchy and unusual side dish.

Helpful Hints

♦ If butterflied pork chops are not available, any type of pork chop can be used. Be sure to remove visible fat and cook until a meat thermometer reads 160°F.

Countdown

♦ Start barley

♦ Prepare pork ingredients

♦ Finish barley

♦ Make pork

SHOPPING LIST

MEAT
3/4 lb butterflied, boneless,
    center-cut pork loin chops

GROCERY
1 bottle dried rosemary
1 small bottle apple butter
1 small bottle prepared horseradish
1 small package quick-cooking
    pearl barley

PRODUCE
1/2 lb fresh green beans

STAPLES
Olive oil spray
Olive oil
Salt
Black peppercorns

Nutrition Facts:
Pork with Apple Butter
Sauce

Exchanges/Choices
1 Carbohydrate
5 Lean Meat

Calories	295
Calories from Fat 100	
Total Fat	11 g
Saturated Fat	3.9 g
Cholesterol	85 mg
Sodium	90 mg
Carbohydrate	17 g
Dietary Fiber	1 g
Sugars	12 g
Protein	32 g

Pork and Apple Butter Sauce

Preparation time: 7 minutes
Serves 2/Serving size: 1/2 recipe

	Olive oil spray
3/4	lb butterflied, boneless, center-cut pork loin chops
2	tsp dried rosemary
	Salt and freshly ground black pepper
1/4	cup apple butter
2	tsp horseradish

1. Heat a medium-size nonstick skillet over medium-high heat and spray with olive oil spray.

2. Remove fat from pork and sprinkle with rosemary. Press rosemary into chops on both sides. Add to skillet and brown 2 minutes. Turn and brown second side 2 minutes. Sprinkle cooked side with salt and pepper to taste.

3. Lower heat to medium low, cover, and cook 2 minutes. A meat thermometer should read 160°F.

4. Mix apple butter and horseradish together. Place pork chops on individual dinner plates and pour pan juices on top. Serve apple butter on the side.

Nutrition Facts:
Quick Barley and
Green Beans

Exchanges/Choices
2 1/2 Starch
1 Vegetable
1/2 Fat

Calories	190
Calories from Fat	35
Total Fat	4 g
Saturated Fat	<1 g
Cholesterol	0 mg
Sodium	0 mg
Carbohydrate	35 g
Dietary Fiber	7 g
Sugars	2 g
Protein	6 g

Quick Barley and Green Beans

Preparation time: 15 minutes
Serves 2/Serving size: 1/2 recipe

1	cup water
1/2	cup quick-cooking pearl barley
1/2	lb trimmed fresh green beans (about 2 cups)
1/2	Tbsp olive oil
	Salt and freshly ground black pepper

1. Bring water to a boil in a medium-size saucepan over high heat. Add barley and lower heat to medium. Cover and boil 5 minutes.

2. Add green beans and continue to cook, covered, 5 minutes.

3. Remove from heat and let stand 5 minutes.

4. Add olive oil and salt and pepper to taste. Mix well.

Ham, Mushroom, and Onion Pizza

with Spinach Salad

This quick and easy pizza is better than delivery in so many ways. The tortilla makes a wonderfully light and crispy crust and the toppings are tasty alternatives to plain cheese and pepperoni. The salad with walnuts rounds out the meal.

Helpful Hints

◆ Any type of sliced mushrooms can be used.

◆ If frozen onion is not available, slice an onion in the microwave and cook on high for 1 minute.

◆ Use nonstick foil to keep tortillas from sticking to foil.

Countdown

◆ Preheat broiler

◆ Make pizza

◆ Assemble salad

SHOPPING LIST

DAIRY
1 small package part-skim milk
   mozzarella cheese

DELI
8 oz lean sliced ham

GROCERY
1 small package 8-inch
   whole-wheat tortillas
1 small can/jar no-salt-added
   tomato sauce
1 small package broken walnuts
1 package frozen, diced, or
   chopped onion

PRODUCE
1 small package sliced baby
   bello mushrooms
1 bag washed ready-to-eat spinach

STAPLES
Reduced-fat oil and vinegar
   salad dressing

Ham, Mushroom, and Onion Pizza

Preparation time: 7 minutes
Serves 2/Serving size: 1/2 recipe

 2 8-inch whole-wheat tortillas
1/2 cup no-salt-added tomato sauce
 1 cup, frozen, diced, or chopped onion
1/2 cup sliced baby bello mushrooms
 8 oz lean sliced ham
 1 oz part-skim milk mozzarella cheese (about 3 Tbsp)

1. Preheat broiler. Line a baking tray with foil.

2. Place tortillas on foil and spread with tomato sauce. Place onion and mushrooms on top. Broil 5 inches from heat for 3 minutes. Remove from broiler.

3. Tear ham into bite-sized pieces and place on top. Sprinkle mozzarella over pizzas and broil 2 minutes.

Nutrition Facts:
Ham, Mushroom, and Onion Pizza

Exchanges/Choices
1 1/2 Starch
2 Vegetable
3 Lean Meat
1 Fat

Calories	350
Calories from Fat	100
Total Fat	11 g
Saturated Fat	3.3 g
Cholesterol	65 mg
Sodium	1,730 mg
Carbohydrate	31 g
Dietary Fiber	4 g
Sugars	7 g
Protein	30 g

Spinach Salad

Preparation time: 2 minutes
Serves 2/Serving size: 1/2 recipe

 4 cups washed ready-to-eat spinach
 2 Tbsp reduced-fat oil and vinegar salad dressing
 2 Tbsp broken walnuts

1. Place spinach in salad bowl and toss with dressing. Sprinkle walnuts on top.

Nutrition Facts:
Spinach Salad

Exchanges/Choices
1 Vegetable
1 1/2 Fat

Calories	90
Calories from Fat	70
Total Fat	8 g
Saturated Fat	<1 g
Cholesterol	0 mg
Sodium	190 mg
Carbohydrate	4 g
Dietary Fiber	2 g
Sugars	1 g
Protein	3 g

Balsamic Veal

with Linguine with Broccoli

It takes only minutes to make a sweet and savory sauce for veal. The secret is sweet balsamic vinegar.

Helpful Hints

◆ Fresh linguine can be found in most supermarkets. Dried linguine can be used. It will take about 8 minutes to cook instead of 3 minutes.

◆ Thin boneless skinless chicken cutlets can be used instead of veal.

◆ Minced garlic in jars can be found in the produce department of the supermarket. If preferred, two large garlic cloves can be used.

Countdown

◆ Boil water for linguine

◆ Make veal

◆ Finish linguine and broccoli

SHOPPING LIST

MEAT
3/4 lb veal cutlets

GROCERY
1 small package frozen,
    diced, or chopped onion
1 small package fresh
    whole-wheat linguine

PRODUCE
1/2 lb broccoli florets
1 small jar minced garlic

STAPLES

Balsamic vinegar
Olive oil
Salt
Black peppercorns

Balsamic Veal

Nutrition Facts:
Balsamic Veal

Exchanges/Choices
1 Carbohydrate
5 Lean Meat

Calories	280
Calories from Fat	65
Total Fat	7 g
Saturated Fat	2.1 g
Cholesterol	135 mg
Sodium	75 mg
Carbohydrate	15 g
Dietary Fiber	1 g
Sugars	7 g
Protein	38 g

Preparation time: 5 minutes
Serves 2/Serving size: 1/2 recipe

- 1 tsp olive oil
- 1 cup frozen diced onion
- 2 tsp minced garlic
- 3/4 lb veal cutlets
  Salt and freshly ground pepper
- 1/4 cup balsamic vinegar
- 1/2 cup water

1. Boil large pot of water for linguine.

2. Heat olive oil in a medium-size nonstick skillet over medium-high heat. Sauté onion and garlic for 2 minutes.

3. Flatten veal with bottom of heavy pan, add to skillet, and sauté 1 minute on each side. Remove and sprinkle with salt and pepper to taste.

4. Raise heat to high, and add balsamic vinegar and 1/2 cup water. Reduce liquid by half, typically about 1 minute.

5. Return veal to pan and warm through, about 30 seconds. Remove from heat. Serve veal and sauce over linguine.

Linguine with Broccoli

Nutrition Facts:
Linguine with Broccoli

Exchanges/Choices
2 Starch
1 Vegetable
1/2 Fat

Calories	210
Calories from Fat	35
Total Fat	4 g
Saturated Fat	<1 g
Cholesterol	0 mg
Sodium	140 mg
Carbohydrate	36 g
Dietary Fiber	5 g
Sugars	3 g
Protein	10 g

Preparation time: 5 minutes
Serves 2/Serving size: 1/2 recipe

- 1/2 lb broccoli florets (about 3 cups)
- 4 oz fresh whole-wheat linguine
- 1 tsp olive oil
  Salt and freshly ground black pepper

1. Bring a large saucepan with 3–4 quarts water to a boil.

2. Add linguine and broccoli to boiling water. Boil 3 minutes. Drain.

3. Toss with 1 tsp olive oil. Add salt and pepper to taste.

Beef Skillet Supper

Sirloin steak remains juicy and tender in this Asian-inspired one-pot meal.

Helpful Hints

◆ Fresh angel hair pasta can be used instead of Chinese noodles.

◆ Two large garlic cloves, crushed, can be used instead of the minced garlic.

◆ Trimmed snow peas can be found in the produce section of many supermarkets. Use trimmed green beans or other green vegetable if snow peas are not available.

Countdown

◆ Assemble ingredients

◆ Complete recipe

SHOPPING LIST

MEAT
8 oz sirloin steak

GROCERY
1 small bottle orange juice
1 small bottle ground ginger

PRODUCE
1 jar minced garlic
1 package shredded cabbage
1/4 lb trimmed snow peas
1 package fresh or steamed
    Chinese egg noodles

STAPLES
Lite soy sauce
Sesame oil
Salt
Black peppercorns

Nutrition Facts:
Beef Skillet Supper

Exchanges/Choices
2 1/2 Starch
3 Vegetable
3 Lean Meat
2 Fat

Calories	495
Calories from Fat	155
Total Fat	17 g
Saturated Fat	3.1 g
Cholesterol	95 mg
Sodium	765 mg
Carbohydrate	54 g
Dietary Fiber	7 g
Sugars	15 g
Protein	37 g

Beef Skillet Supper

Preparation time: 8 minutes
Serves 2/Serving size: 1/2 recipe

> 4 tsp minced garlic
> 2 Tbsp light soy sauce
> 1/2 cup orange juice
> 1/2 cup water
> 4 tsp ground ginger
> 4 tsp sesame oil, divided use
> 8 oz sirloin steak, fat removed, cut into 1/2-inch strips
>   Salt and freshly ground black pepper
> 1/4 lb fresh or steamed Chinese egg noodles
> 4 cups shredded cabbage
> 1/4 lb trimmed snow peas (about 2 cups)

1. Mix garlic, soy sauce, orange juice, water, and ginger together.

2. Heat 2 teaspoon oil in a large, nonstick skillet over medium-high heat. Add steak strips and sauté 1 minute, turn and cook 1 minute. Remove from heat and sprinkle with salt and pepper to taste.

3. Add the sauce, noodles, cabbage, and snow peas to the skillet. Bring to a boil and cook 3 minutes. Return the meat to the skillet and cook 1 minute.

4. Remove from heat and stir in the remaining 2 teaspoons of oil. Serve on two dinner plates.

Recipe Index

Subject Index

A

Almonds, toasting, 51

Apples, 35

Avocados, ripening, 67

B

Basil, 89

Beans

    black, 135

    cannellini, 203

    navy, 203

    refried, 79

    small red kidney, 189

Beef. *see* Steak

Bijol, 165

Blueberries, frozen, 24

Breads, *xiv*

    hot dog buns, whole wheat, 61

    pita bread, 81

Breakfast, *xv–xviii*, 1–31

Broccoli, 171

Bronzing, 179

Brown rice, *xii*, 162, 183

Buying tips, *xi–xii*

C

Carambola (star fruit), 168

Cereals, *xiv*

Cheese

    cheddar, 22

    feta, 81

    Gorgonzola, 14

    Monterey jack, 79

    Parmesan, *xi,* 129

    reduced-fat, 22, 79

Chicken

    cooked chicken strips, 51, 67, 181

        flattening, 96, 179

        meat thermometer readings, 96, 193

    roasted chicken breast, 187

    for stir-fry, 185

Chinese noodles, 147, 213

Chives, 195

Cilantro, 75

Coffee slush, 105

Coleslaw, prepared, 73, 174

Condiments, *xiv*

Cooking methods, *xii–xiii*

    bronzing, 179

    chicken, flattening, 96

    fish, *xiii*

    frittatas, 6

    kabobs, 117, 162

    omelets, 6, 12, 16

    pasta, *xiii*

    pork, 141

    rice, 162

    squash, 138

About the American Diabetes Association

American Diabetes Association Complete Guide to Diabetes, 4th Edition

by American Diabetes Association

Have all the tips and information on diabetes that you need close at hand. The world's largest collection of diabetes self-care tips, techniques, and tricks for solving diabetes-related problems is back in its fourth edition, and it's bigger and better than ever before.

Order no. 4809-04; New low price $19.95

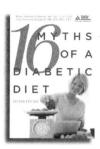

16 Myths of a Diabetic Diet, 2nd Edition

by Karen Hanson Chalmers, MS, RD, LDN, CDE, and Amy Peterson Campbell, MS, RD, LDN, CDE

16 Myths of a Diabetic Diet will tell you the truth about diabetes and how to eat when you have diabetes. Learn what the most common myths about diabetes meal plans are, where they came from, and how to overcome them. Let experts Karen Chalmers and Amy Campbell show you how to create and follow a healthy, enjoyable way of eating.

Order no. 4829-02; Price $14.95

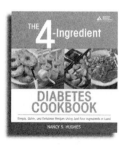

The 4-Ingredient Diabetes Cookbook

by Nancy S. Hughes

Making delicious meals doesn't have to be complicated, time-consuming, or expensive. You can create satisfying dishes using just four ingredients (or even fewer)! Make the most of your time and money. You'll be amazed at how much you can prepare with just a few simple ingredients.

Order no. 4662-01; Price $16.95

The Big Book of Diabetic Desserts

by Jackie Mills, MS, RD

This first-ever collection of guilty pleasures proves that people with diabetes never have to say no to dessert again. Packed with familiar favorites and some delicious new surprises, *The Big Book of Diabetic Desserts* has more than 150 tantalizing treats that will satisfy any sweet tooth.

Order no. 4664-01; Price $18.95

To order these and other great American Diabetes Association titles,
call **1-800-232-6733**, or visit **http://store.diabetes.org**.
American Diabetes Association titles are also available in bookstores nationwide.

About the American Diabetes Association

The American Diabetes Association is the nation's leading voluntary health organization supporting diabetes research, information, and advocacy. Its mission is to prevent and cure diabetes and to improve the lives of all people affected by diabetes. The American Diabetes Association is the leading publisher of comprehensive diabetes information. Its huge library of practical and authoritative books for people with diabetes covers every aspect of self-care—cooking and nutrition, fitness, weight control, medications, complications, emotional issues, and general self-care.

To order American Diabetes Association books: Call 1-800-232-6733 or log on to http://store.diabetes.org

To join the American Diabetes Association: Call 1-800-806-7801 or log on to www.diabetes.org/membership

For more information about diabetes or ADA programs and services: Call 1-800-342-2383. E-mail: AskADA@diabetes.org or log on to www.diabetes.org

To locate an ADA/NCQA Recognized Provider of quality diabetes care in your area: www.ncqa.org/dprp

To find an ADA Recognized Education Program in your area: Call 1-800-342-2383. www.diabetes.org/for-health-professionals-and-scientists/recognition/edrecognition.jsp

To join the fight to increase funding for diabetes research, end discrimination, and improve insurance coverage: Call 1-800-342-2383. www.diabetes.org/advocacy-and-legalresources/advocacy.jsp

To find out how you can get involved with the programs in your community: Call 1-800-342-2383. See below for program Web addresses.

- **AMERICAN DIABETES MONTH**: educational activities aimed at those diagnosed with diabetes—month of November. www.diabetes.org/communityprograms-and-localevents/americandiabetesmonth.jsp

- **AMERICAN DIABETES ALERT**: annual public awareness campaign to find the undiagnosed—held the fourth Tuesday in March. www.diabetes.org/communityprograms-and-localevents/americandiabetesalert.jsp

- **AMERICAN DIABETES ASSOCIATION LATINO INITIATIVE**: diabetes awareness program targeted to the Latino community. www.diabetes.org/communityprograms-and-localevents/latinos.jsp

- **AFRICAN AMERICAN PROGRAM**: diabetes awareness program targeted to the African American community. www.diabetes.org/communityprograms-and-localevents/africanamericans.jsp

- **AWAKENING THE SPIRIT**: Pathways to Diabetes Prevention & Control: diabetes awareness program targeted to the Native American community. www.diabetes.org/communityprograms-and-localevents/nativeamericans.jsp

To find out about an important research project regarding type 2 diabetes: www.diabetes.org/diabetes-research/research-home.jsp

To obtain information on making a planned gift or charitable bequest: Call 1-888-700-7029. www.wpg.cc/stl/CDA/homepage/1,1006,509,00.html

To make a donation or memorial contribution: Call 1-800-342-2383. www.diabetes.org/support-the-cause/make-a-donation.jsp

American Diabetes Association.
Cure • Care • Commitment®